shifra stein's

day trips® from
san antonio

Praise for previous editions:

*"If the idea of traveling Texas this summer appeals to you but
you don't have a week or two to devote to wandering the farm-to-market roads
searching for interesting Lone Star locales, there is a solution:* Day Trips®.*"*

—San Antonio Current

*"*Day Trips® *is a very user-friendly guide . . . good for stashing in the car
for those spontaneous Sunday drives."*

—Austin Chronicle

*"Your family loves to travel but you have limited time, energy, and/or budget.
Have we found the book for you.* Day Trips®.*"*

—Austin Child

help us keep this guide up to date

Every effort has been made by the authors and editors to make this guide as accurate and useful as possible. However, many changes can occur after a guide is published—establishments close, phone numbers change, hiking trails are rerouted, facilities come under new management, and so on.

We would love to hear from you concerning your experiences with this guide and how you feel it could be improved and be kept up to date. While we may not be able to respond to all comments and suggestions, we'll take them to heart, and we'll make certain to share them with the authors. Please send your comments and suggestions to the following address:

The Globe Pequot Press
Reader Response/Editorial Department
P.O. Box 480
Guilford, CT 06437
Or you may e-mail us at: editorial@GlobePequot.com

Thanks for your input, and happy travels!

INSIDERS' GUIDE®

day trips® series

shifra stein's

day trips® from san antonio

third edition

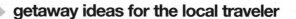

getaway ideas for the local traveler

paris permenter

and

john bigley

INSIDERS' GUIDE®

GUILFORD, CONNECTICUT
AN IMPRINT OF THE GLOBE PEQUOT PRESS

The prices and rates listed in this guidebook were confirmed at press time. We recommend, however, that you call establishments before traveling to obtain current information.

To buy books in quantity for corporate use or incentives, call **(800) 962–0973, ext. 4551,** or e-mail **premiums@GlobePequot.com.**

INSIDERS' GUIDE ®

Copyright © 1997, 2000, 2004, 2006 Morris Book Publishing, LLC
Copyright © 1992, 1995 Two Lane Press, Inc.

Insiders' Guide is a registered trademark of Morris Book Publishing, LLC.
Day Trips is a registered trademark.

Text design by Linda R. Loiewski
Maps by XNR Productions Inc. © Morris Book Publishing, LLC
Spot photography throughout © Richard Cummins/SuperStock

ISSN: 1545-0333
ISBN-13: 978-0-7627-3868-7
ISBN-10: 0-7627-3868-5

Manufactured in the United States of America
Third Edition/First Printing

contents

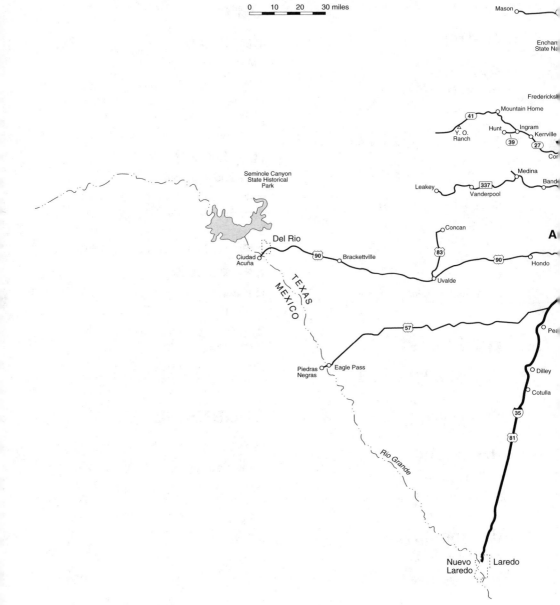

0   10   20   30 miles

Mason

Enchan
State Na

Fredericks

Mountain Home

(41)
Y. O.
Ranch
Hunt   Ingram
(39)   Kerrville
(27)
Cor

Medina

Seminole Canyon
State Historical
Park
Leakey   (337)   Band
Vanderpool

Concan

A

Del Rio
(90)   Brackettville   (83)   (90)   Hondo

Ciudad
Acuña

TEXAS

MEXICO

Uvalde

(57)   Pea

Dilley

Piedras   Eagle Pass
Negras

Cotulla

(35)

(81)

Rio Grande

Nuevo   Laredo
Laredo

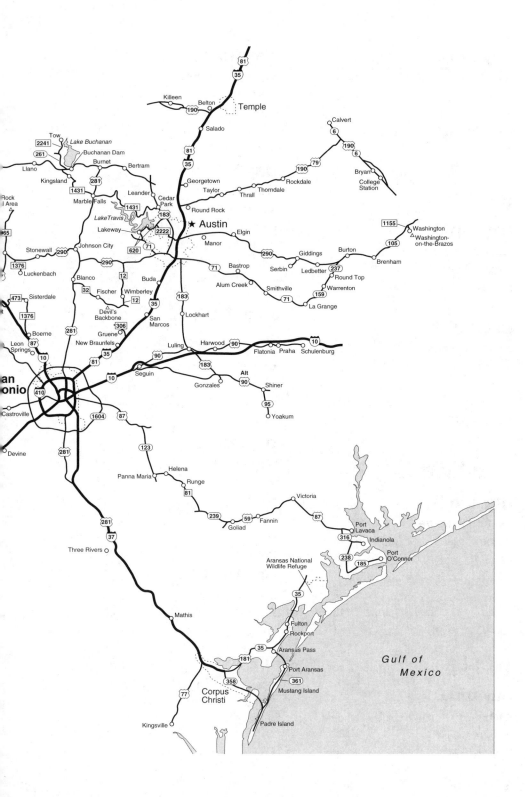

introduction

Welcome to San Antonio—the Alamo City and the gateway to South Texas.

Most people have a mental image of Texas as miles of rugged, uncivilized land where the outlines of cattle and lonely windmills stretch above the horizon. But that's just one side of the Lone Star State, also known as the "land of contrast." Texas also boasts high-tech cities, piney woods, sandy beaches, rolling hills, and fertile farmland—much of it within a two-hour drive of San Antonio.

With its semitropical climate and lush vegetation, San Antonio offers a south-of-the-border atmosphere with north-of-the-border amenities. Because the city lies at the juncture of the Hill Country, farmland, and brush country that stretches to the Mexican border, *Day Trips from San Antonio* spans terrain ranging from farmland to rocky hills. This difference in topography is the result of an ancient earthquake that created the Balcones Fault, which runs north to south. The fault line, slightly west of I–35, forms the dividing line between the eastern agricultural region and what is known as the Hill Country to the west.

The region covered in *Day Trips from San Antonio* is as diverse as the more than thirty cultures that helped found the state. In fact, the influences of these pioneers are still apparent today in the many festivals and ethnic foods that vacationers come here to enjoy. You can head to the urban areas of Austin or Corpus Christi, or to small towns where it's not uncommon to hear German, Czech, Spanish, or even Alsatian spoken on the street. You also can get away from it all with a quiet walk along miles of undeveloped beach on Padre Island, or take a bird-watching cruise along the Intracoastal Waterway of the Rockport-Fulton area. Most day trip recommendations also include information about overnight accommodations to make your visit more relaxing and unhurried, so you'll have plenty of time to watch a Texas-size sunset or sunrise over the Gulf waters.

Many of the attractions lie along the route taken by the 350,000 "Winter Texans" who flock here during the cooler months. So whether you're heading for the Rio Grande Valley, the coast, or the Mexican border, you'll find a wealth of useful tips and information inside. Be sure to check the sections marked "Especially for Winter Texans," as well as Appendix C, which will help you identify special services, festivals, or parks aimed at making you feel right at home.

To get the most out of each day trip, here are some travel tips to keep in mind.

Carry a Road Map. Although we've included directions, it's best to carry a Texas road map as you travel. It's also advisable to carry a county map for a better look at farm-to-market (FM) roads and ranch roads (RR). You can get brochures on Texas attractions and a free copy of the *Texas State Travel Guide* from the Texas Department of Transportation, P.O. Box 5064, Austin, TX 78763-5064, or by calling (800) 8888–TEX or visiting www.traveltex.com. The travel guide is available in print and online. The guide is coded to a free Texas state map provided by the Highway Department. State maps are also available from any of the tourist information centers located on routes into Texas and at the Texas State Capitol in Austin. The tourist information centers are open daily, except for Thanksgiving, Christmas, and New Year's Day.

The expansiveness of Texas sets it apart from other states. Note the scale of the map. With 266,807 square miles of land, Texas is the second largest state in the country. One inch on the state road map spans 23 miles.

Driving varies with terrain: The two-hour time limit that constitutes a "day trip" here has been stretched for the westernmost trips in this book. You won't find many towns en route from San Antonio to the Mexican border, and there's little traffic to slow your drive. To the east, population is more dense, and day trips involve quiet, slow drives along farm-to-market and ranch roads.

For questions about travel in Texas, call (800) 452–9292.

using this travel guide

Highway designations: *Federal highways are designated US. State routes use TX for Texas. Farm-to-market roads are indicated by FM, and ranch roads are labeled RR. County roads (which are not on the Texas state map) are identified as such.*

Hours: *In most cases, hours are omitted in the listings because they are subject to frequent changes. Instead, phone numbers appear for obtaining up-to-date information.*

Restaurants: *Restaurant prices are designated as $$$ (Expensive: $20 and more per person); $$ (Moderate: $10–$19); and $ (Inexpensive: less than $10).*

Accommodations: *Room prices are designated as $$$ (Expensive: more than $100 for a standard room); $$ (Moderate: $50–$100); and $ (Inexpensive: less than $50).*

For brochures and maps on San Antonio area attractions, call (800) 447–3327 or (201) 207–6700; write San Antonio Convention and Visitors Bureau, P.O. Box 2277, San Antonio, TX 78298; or see www.sanantoniocvb.com.

Avoid Midday Heat. In summer, the Texas heat is hotter than sizzling fajitas. In warm weather, it's best to drive in the early morning hours or after sunset. If you are traveling with pets, never leave them in an enclosed car; temperatures soar to ovenlike heights in just minutes.

Heed Road Signs and Weather Warnings. Always be on the lookout for road signs, and if you see a notice, observe it. Obey flash flood warnings: A sudden rainstorm can turn a wash into a deadly torrent. The Hill Country north and west of San Antonio is the most dangerous region for flash flooding. Never cross a flooded roadway; it may be deeper than you think.

Watch Out for Stray Livestock. When driving through open-ranch cattle country on farm-to-market or ranch roads, be on the lookout for livestock and deer wandering across the road, especially near dusk.

You'll find that Texans are friendly folk who wave on country roads and nod as they pass you on the sidewalk. Talk to local citizens as you wind through the back roads for even more travel tips and a firsthand look at the varied cultures that make up the pieces of your journey.

north

day trip 01

north

kodak country:
blanco, fischer, devil's backbone
scenic drive, wimberley

blanco

To reach Blanco, follow US 281 north of San Antonio past miles of cattle ranches and Hill Country vistas. Formerly a "Wild West" kind of town, the community was originally the seat of Blanco County. Although the county seat eventually moved to nearby Johnson City, where it remains today, local residents have restored Blanco's old limestone courthouse, located at the intersection of US 281 and TX 165. Stop by for brochures and shopping.

Around the courthouse square are several art galleries and antiques shops aimed at weekend visitors, many of whom stop to camp at the Blanco River State Park south of town.

where to go

Blanco State Park. South of Blanco on US 281; (830) 833–4333; www.tpwd.state.tx.us. During the depression, the Civilian Conservation Corps built two stone dams, a group pavilion, stone picnic tables, and an arched bridge in this 104-acre riverside park. Today the park is popular with swimmers, anglers, and campers. Fee.

Blanco Bowling Club. East of the square on Fourth Street; (830) 833–4416. Housed in 1940s buildings, the bowling club and the adjacent cafe have changed little with the passing years. The nine-pin game is still set up by hand as it has been for generations. The bowling

club opens at 7:30 P.M. Monday through Friday (except during football season, when everyone's at the Friday-night high school game). To bowl you must be a league member. Fee.

where to eat

Blanco Bowling Club Cafe. East of the square on Fourth Street; (830) 833–4416. This is
a traditional Texas diner, with a linoleum floor and Formica tables, and chairs filled with locals
who come here at the same time every day. Chicken-fried steak is the specialty; on Friday
nights there's a catfish plate as well. Stop by in the morning for huge glazed twists and
doughnuts made from scratch. Open daily for breakfast, lunch, and dinner. $.

north day trip 01

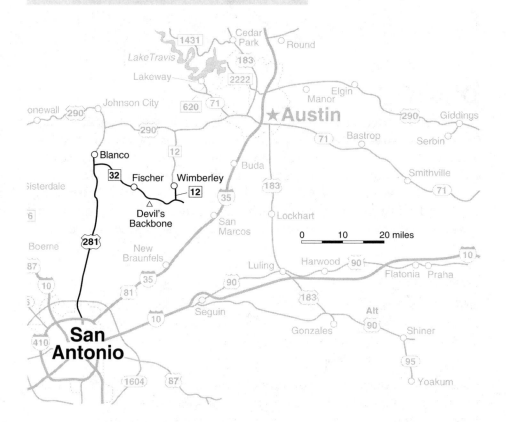

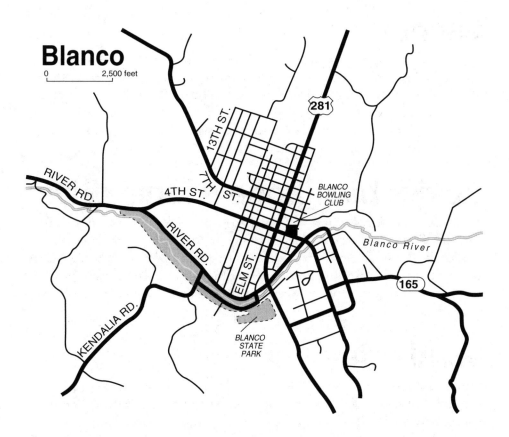

Blanco

0　　　　2,500 feet

musical chairs with the county seat

Built in 1888, the former Blanco County Courthouse has been one of the most used buildings in the county—for everything except as a courthouse, that is. The year after its construction, an election moved the county seat to Johnson City. The courthouse was used a total of four years for its original purpose, then it went into a long career of different uses. For two different periods, the building served as a schoolhouse; it also became a bank. Later it served the community as a town hall, library, opera house, and even the office of the local newspaper. From 1937 to 1961 the building served as a hospital, but later it became a Wild West museum and then a barbecue restaurant. Today the building houses the visitor center and is used for community events.

fischer

It's just a short, winding drive through the country from Blanco to the tiny hamlet of Fischer. Retrace your drive south on US 281 for a couple of miles to the intersection of RR 32. Take a left and enjoy a quiet ride through miles of ranch land and rolling hills.

Fischer is on the left side of the road. Today not much remains of this community, just a post office, complete with an old-fashioned postmaster's cage and tiny brass mailboxes. Inside, enormous counters span the length of the dark and musty building.

devil's backbone scenic drive

The Devil's Backbone scenic drive stretches along RR 32 from Fischer to the intersection of RR 12, your turnoff for Wimberley. There aren't any steep climbs or stomach-churning look-outs; a high ridge of hills provides a gentle drive with excellent views along the way. There's very little traffic, plus a beautiful picnic spot on the left, just a few miles out of Fischer. This stretch of road is often cited as one of the most scenic drives in Texas and is well known for its fall color.

wimberley

At the end of the Devil's Backbone, RR 32 intersects with RR 12. Take a left on RR 12, and then drive 5 miles. This road drops from the steep ridge to the fertile valley that's home to the Blanco River and Cypress Creek.

Wimberley's history goes back to the 1850s, when a resourceful Texas Revolution veteran named William Winters opened a mill here. As was tradition at the time, he named the new community Winters' Mill. When Winters died, John Cade bought the mill, and the town became Cade's Mill. Finally in 1870, a wealthy Llano man named Pleasant Wimberley rode into town. Tired of Indian raids on his horses in Llano, he moved in, bought the mill, and changed the town's name one last time.

The small town of Wimberley is one of those "shop 'til you drop" kinds of places. Even with only 3,800 residents, the town boasts dozens of specialty stores, art galleries and studios, and accommodations ranging from river resorts to historic bed-and-breakfasts.

Wimberley is a quiet place except when the shops open their doors on Fridays, Mondays, and weekends. The busiest time to visit is the first Saturday of the month, from April through December. This is Market Day, when more than 400 vendors set up to sell antiques, collectibles, and arts and crafts.

Many visitors come to enjoy the town's two water sources: the Blanco River and clear, chilly Cypress Creek. Both are filled with inner-tubers and swimmers during hot summer months. The waterways provide a temporary home for campers and vacationers who stay in resorts and cabins along the shady water's edge.

where to go

Wimberley Chamber of Commerce. Wimberley North Shopping Center, RR 12 past Cypress Creek; (512) 847–2201; www.wimberley.org. Stop by the chamber offices on weekdays to load up on brochures, maps, and friendly shopping tips.

Pioneertown. 7-A Ranch Resort, 1 mile west of RR 12 on County Road 178, at the intersection of County Road 179; (512) 847–2517; www.7aranchresort.com. See a medicine show, tour a general store museum, or spend some time at the town jail in this Wild West village. There's also an old log fort, cowboy shows, and a western cafe. A narrow-gauge railway winds 1 mile along the Wimberley Valley. For a closer look at the countryside, you can also arrange for a trail ride and, from the saddle, experience the area like a true pioneer. Open weekends year-round and daily during the summer months. Fee.

where to shop

Like nearby Blanco, Wimberley is home to many artists who've relocated to Texas's serene Hill Country. Specialty shops abound, selling everything from imports to sculpture and antiques. Arts and crafts are especially well represented. Plan to shop Friday through Monday. Some stores are open all week, but most close midweek, especially during cooler months.

Rancho Deluxe. On the square, 14010 RR 12; (877) 847–9570 or (512) 847–9570; www.ranchodeluxe.net. Bring the cowboy look to your home with this shop's western merchandise. You'll find everything from spurs to Mexican sideboards, and from horns to handcrafted furniture. Open daily.

Teeks Gallery. On the square; (512) 847–8868. This shop features an eclectic blend of art, books, jewelry, and stationery.

Wimberley Glass Works. 1.6 miles south of the square on RR 12; (512) 847–9348; www.wgw.com. Watch demonstrations on the art of hand-blown glass and shop for one-of-a-kind creations. Open daily.

Wimberley Stained Glass Shop. On the square; (512) 847–3930. Highlighted by handcrafted Tiffany lamp reproductions, this shop also features custom-leaded doors, window panels, and sun catchers.

where to stay

Wimberley is filled with bed-and-breakfast accommodations that range from historic homes in town to ranches in the surrounding Hill Country to camps alongside Cypress Creek. For information on these many accommodations, give one of the reservations services a call: Bed and Breakfast of Wimberley, (800) 827–1913; Hill Country Accommodations, (800) 926–5028; All Wimberley Lodging, (800) 460–3909, www.texashillcountrylodging.com; and Texas Hill Country Retreats, (800) 236–9411, www.texashillco.com. For brochures on Wimberley's other accommodations, call the chamber of commerce at (512) 847–2201.

day trip 02

north

lbj country:

johnson city, stonewall, luckenbach, fredericksburg, enchanted rock state natural area

johnson city

The Lyndon B. Johnson National Historic Park takes in two areas: Johnson City and the LBJ Ranch. To reach Johnson City, follow US 281 north to Blanco (see North Day Trip 1 in this section for attractions along this stretch of road).

LBJ brought the attention of the world to his hometown, located 14 miles north from Blanco on US 281. The most popular stop here is the LBJ Boyhood Home, managed by the U.S. Park Service. LBJ was five years old in 1913 when his family moved from their country home near the Pedernales River to this simple frame house. The visitor center provides information on this location, nearby Johnson Settlement, and other LBJ attractions. Park admission is free of charge, a stipulation of the late president.

where to go

LBJ National Historic Park. South of US 290 at Ninth Street. Park at the visitor center and go inside for brochures and a look at exhibits. From the center you can walk to two historic areas: Johnson Settlement and the LBJ Boyhood Home.

Johnson Settlement. The settlement gives visitors a look at the beginnings of the Johnson legacy. These rustic cabins and outbuildings once belonged to LBJ's grandfather Sam Ealy Johnson and his brother Tom. The two cattle drivers lived a rugged life in the Hill Country

north day trip 02

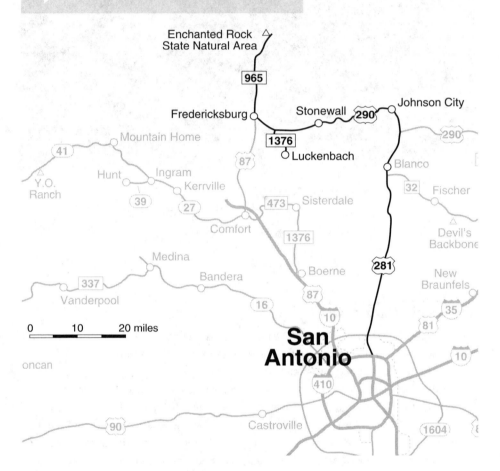

during the 1860s and '70s. An exhibit center tells this story in pictures and artifacts. You also can tour the brothers' cabins and see costumed docents carrying out nineteenth-century chores. Open daily. Free.

LBJ Boyhood Home. Next to the Johnson Settlement. LBJ was a schoolboy when his family moved here in 1913. The home is still furnished with the Johnsons' belongings. Guided tours run every half hour. Open daily. Free.

The Exotic Resort Zoo. Four miles north of Johnson City on US 281; (830) 868–4357; www.zooexotics.com. Unusual species (including many endangered animals) roam across the 137 acres of wooded Hill Country. In this park, leave the driving to someone else and enjoy a guided ride aboard a safari truck. Professional guides conduct tours of the ranch and provide you with information on animal behavior and other topics as you feed the friendly park residents. After the tour, you can see some wildlife up close at the petting zoo. Kids enjoy petting child-size miniature donkeys, baby deer, llamas, baby elks, and even a kangaroo at this special area. Open daily. Fee.

Pedernales Falls State Park. About 9 miles east on FM 2766; (830) 868–7304; www.tpwd.state.tx.us. A favorite summer getaway, this 4,800-acre state park is highlighted with gently cascading waterfalls. Swimming, fishing, camping, and hiking available. Open daily. Fee.

where to eat

Uncle Kunkel's Bar B Q. 208 US 281 South; (830) 868–0251. For years the Kunkels did the catering for the LBJ Ranch, and today they prepare their award-winning pork ribs, brisket, and sausage for the public. Have a plate of smoked meats with side dishes of potato salad, coleslaw, or pinto beans, followed by a slice of homemade pie. $.

where to stay

The Exotic Zoo Bed and Breakfast. US 281; (830) 868–4357; www.zooexotics.com. The Exotic Resort Zoo, known for its guided safari tours and petting zoo, now operates a four-cabin bed-and-breakfast on the property. Two cabins include kitchenettes; they all include access to two swimming pools, a hot tub, barbecue area, and fire pit for evening bonfires. The cabins overlook the animal areas, and guests can also fish on a stocked lake, paying only for those fish caught. There is a seven-day cancellation policy on cabin rentals. $$$.

stonewall

From Johnson City, head west on US 290 to the tiny community of Stonewall, the capital of the Texas peach industry. The road passes through miles of peach orchards, and during early summer, farm-fresh fruit is sold at roadside stands throughout the area. Stonewall is also the home of the LBJ National and State Historic Parks, encompassing the LBJ Ranch.

where to go

LBJ National and State Historic Parks. Located 14 miles west of Johnson City on US 290; (830) 644–2252; www.nps.gov or www.tpwd.state.tx.us. These two combined parks together span approximately 700 acres. The area is comprised of three main sections: the visitor center, the LBJ Ranch and tour, and the Sauer-Beckmann Farm. The most scenic route to the LBJ Park falls along RR 1, paralleling the wide, shallow Pedernales River. (Exit US 290 a few miles east of Stonewall.)

During Johnson's life, the ranch was closed to all but official visitors. In hopes of catching a glimpse of the president, travelers often stopped along RR 1, located across the river from the "Texas White House," the nickname of the Johnsons' home. Today the parks draw visitors from around the world, who come for a look at the history behind the Hill Country, the presidency of LBJ, and a working Texas ranch.

Make your first stop the visitor center for a look at displays on LBJ's life, including mementos of President Johnson's boyhood years. Attached to the visitor center is the Behrens Cabin, a dogtrot-style structure built by a German immigrant in the 1870s. Inside, the home is furnished with household items from more than a century ago.

While you're in the visitor center, sign up for a ninety-minute guided tour of the LBJ Ranch, operated by the National Park Service. Tour buses run from 10:00 A.M. to 4:00 P.M. daily and travel across the president's ranch, making a stop at the one-room Junction School where Johnson began his education. The bus slows down for a photo of the Texas White House, then continues past the president's airstrip and cattle barns. Other stops include a look at the reconstructed birthplace home as well as the family cemetery where the former president is buried.

Near the end of the tour, the bus makes an optional stop at the Sauer-Beckmann Living Historical Farm. The two 1918 farm homes are furnished in period style. Outside, children can have a great time petting the farm animals. From here, it's just a short walk back to the visitor center.

peach fun

Stonewall's called the "Peach Capital of Texas" and every June the town is ripe with fun and festivities. The third weekend of June is set aside for a celebration of the Hill Country's sweetest product at the annual Peach JAMboree, a time when the small community shares its fuzzy treasure. The festivities are genuine Texas fun, from a rodeo with bareback riding, calf roping, team roping, and bull riding to a parade and a baking contest at the fire station. Other activities include a fiddlers' contest (open to competitors), a washer pitching tournament, and, of course, the Gillespie County Peach Queen Pageant. The sweetest event is the Peach Show and Auction, with plenty of prize-winning examples of Stonewall's crop.

Gillespie County, including Stonewall and nearby Fredericksburg, is filled with orchards where you can pick your own peaches. These shady groves yield their fruit until late July and offer a dozen varieties of peaches. The earliest to ripen are the cling peaches, ones whose fruit clings to the pit. As the summer progresses, varieties such as Red Skin, Loring, and Harvest Gold begin to mature.

Although the park does not have overnight facilities, there are two picnic areas and hiking trails for day use. Open daily. Free; fee for bus tour.

Grape Creek Vineyards. Four miles west of Stonewall on US 290; (830) 664–2710; www.grapecreek.com. The fertile land of the Pedernales Valley is a natural for vineyards, and you'll find acres of beautiful grape vines at this winery that produces Cabernet Sauvignon and Chardonnay varieties. The winery is open Tuesday through Sunday from Easter through Labor Day, and Fridays and weekends in winter. Call for tour times. Free.

luckenbach

Waylon Jennings's popular country-western song made this community a Texas institution. The town consists of a shop or two and a small general store serving as a post office, dance hall, beer joint, and general gathering place.

To reach Luckenbach, leave Stonewall on US 290. Turn left on FM 1376 and continue for about 4¼ miles. Don't expect to see signs pointing to the turnoff for Luckenbach Road; they are often stolen as fast as the Highway Department can get them in the ground. After the turn for Grapetown, take the next right down a narrow country road. Luckenbach is just around the bend.

This town was founded in 1852 by Jacob, William, and August Luckenbach. The brothers opened a post office at the site and called it South Grape Creek. In 1886 a man named August Engel reopened the post office and renamed it Luckenbach in honor of the early founders.

The old post office is still there, the walls covered with scrawled names penned by Luckenbach fans. The store sells souvenirs of the town daily. For more information on Luckenbach happenings, call (830) 997–3224.

fredericksburg

Retrace your steps from Luckenbach and continue west on US 290 to Fredericksburg, once the edge of the frontier and home to brave German pioneers. These first inhabitants faced many hardships, including hostile Comanche Indians; now the town is a favorite with antiques shoppers, history buffs, and fans of good German food.

US 290 runs through the heart of the downtown district, becoming Main Street within the city limits. Originally the street was designed to be large enough to allow a wagon and team of mules to turn around in the center of town. Today, Main Street is filled with shoppers who come to explore the stores and restaurants of downtown Fredericksburg. Stop by the visitor center at 106 North Adams for brochures and maps.

Fredericksburg welcomes all visitors—just look at the street signs for proof. Starting at the Adams Street intersection, head east on Main Street and take the first letter of every intersecting street name: They spell "ALL WELCOME." Drive west on Main Street starting after the Adams Street intersection, and the first letters of the intersecting streets spell "COME BACK."

That welcoming spirit extends from the excellent restaurants to the unique boutique shops that line Main Street to hundreds of cozy bed-and-breakfast establishments that dot Gillespie County. Unlike traditional bed-and-breakfasts, where the owners or managers reside on the premises, guest houses are usually managed by a reservation service. After checking in with the service, guests receive directions and keys. Breakfast, which may range from a simple continental meal to a spread of sausage wraps and homemade pastries, often awaits in the refrigerator. But perhaps nowhere else is the visitor's welcome so obvious as at Fredericksburg's many festivals.

Fredericksburg is a prime destination for day-trippers looking for antiques, gifts, books, Texas wines, and one-of-a-kind purchases. The shops along Fredericksburg's Main Street and nearby side streets offer travelers a weekend bursting with shopping opportunities, no matter what their tastes.

where to go

Fredericksburg Chamber of Commerce. 302 East Austin; (888) 997–3600 or (830) 997–6523; www.fredericksburg-texas.com. Stop by the chamber offices for brochures, maps, and information on a self-guided walking tour of historic downtown buildings, many of which now house shops and restaurants. The staff here also can direct you to bed-and-breakfast facilities in the area. Open Monday through Saturday. Free.

National Museum of the Pacific War. 340 East Main Street; (830) 997–4379; www .nimitz-museum.org. This historic park (formerly the Admiral Nimitz State Historical Park) is composed of several sections: the former Nimitz Steamboat Hotel, the Garden of Peace, the Pacific History Walk, and the George Bush Gallery of the Pacific War.

This complex was first named for Adm. Chester Nimitz, World War II commander in chief of the Pacific (CinCPac), Fredericksburg's most famous resident. He commanded two-and-a-half million troops from the time he assumed command eighteen days after the attack on Pearl Harbor until the Japanese surrendered.

The Nimitz name was well known here even years earlier. Having spent time in the merchant marines, Capt. Charles H. Nimitz, the admiral's grandfather, decided to build a hotel here, adding a structure much like a ship's bridge to the front of his establishment. Built in 1852, the Nimitz Steamboat Hotel catered to guests who enjoyed a room, a meal, and the use of an outdoor bathhouse.

Today the former hotel houses a three-story museum honoring Admiral Nimitz and Fredericksburg's early residents. Many exhibits are devoted to World War II, including several that illustrate the Pacific campaign. In addition to displays that record the building's past, several early hotel rooms, the hotel kitchen, and the bathhouse have been restored.

Behind the museum lies the Garden of Peace, a gift from the people of Japan. This classic Japanese garden includes a flowing stream, a raked bed of pebbles and stones representing the sea and the Pacific islands, and a replica of the study used by Admiral Togo, Nimitz's counterpart in the Japanese forces.

Follow the signs from the Garden of Peace for 1 block to the Pacific History Walk. This takes you past a collection of military artifacts including a Nagasaki-type "fat man" atomic bomb case, a Japanese tank, and a restored barge like the one used by Nimitz.

The museum added the 20,000-square-foot George Bush Gallery of the Pacific War. The highlight of this exhibit is a midget submarine captured at Pearl Harbor and a B-25 airplane. These exhibits are located adjacent to the Plaza of the Presidents, an exhibit that

Fredericksburg

0   .5 mile

opened in September 1995 with monuments to ten presidents from FDR to the first President Bush, each of whom had a role in World War II. Open daily. Fee.

Pioneer Museum Complex. 309 West Main Street; (830) 997–2835. This collection of historic old homes includes an 1849 pioneer log home and store, the old First Methodist Church, and a smokehouse and log cabin. Also on the premises you'll see a typical nineteenth-century "Sunday house." Built in Fredericksburg, Sunday houses catered to farmers who would travel long distances to do business in town, often staying the weekend. With the advent of the automobile, such accommodations became obsolete. Today the old Sunday houses scattered throughout the town are used as bed-and-breakfasts, shops, and even private residences. They are easy to identify by their small size and the fact that most have half-story outside staircases. Open Monday through Saturday 10:00 A.M. to 5:00 P.M., Sunday noon to 5:00 P.M. Fee.

Fort Martin Scott Historic Site. 1606 East Main Street, 2 miles east of Fredericksburg on US 290; (830) 997–9895; www.fortmartinscott.com. Established in 1848, this was the first frontier military fort in Texas. Today the original stockade, a guardhouse, and a visitor center with displays on local Indians are open to tour, and historical reenactments keep the history lesson lively. Ongoing archaeological research conducted here offers a glimpse into the fort's past. Reenactments involving costumed Indians, infantrymen, and civilians are scheduled at least once a month. Open Tuesday though Sunday. Fee.

Vereins Kirche Museum. Market Square on Main Street across from the courthouse; (830) 997–7832 or (830) 997–2835. You can't miss this attraction: It's housed in an exact replica of an octagonal structure erected in 1847. Back then the edifice was used as a church, as well as a school, fort, meeting hall, and storehouse. The museum is sometimes called the Coffee Mill (or Die Kaffe-Muehle) Church because of its unusual shape. Exhibits here display Fredericksburg's German heritage, plus Indian artifacts from archaeological digs. Open Monday through Saturday and Sunday afternoon. Free.

Bell Mountain Vineyards. TX 16 North, 14 miles from Fredericksburg; (830) 685–3297; www.bellmountainwine.com. Tour the château-type winery that produces Chardonnay, Reisling, Pinot Noir, and several private reserve estate varieties. Guided tours and tastings are offered every Saturday from March through mid-December. Free.

Fredericksburg Herb Farm. 402 Whitney Street; (800) 259–HERB or (830) 997–8615; www.fredericksburgherbfarm.com. These herb gardens produce everything from teas to potpourris. Tour the grounds, then visit the shop for a look at the final product. A bed-and-breakfast is also located on-site. Open daily (afternoons only on Sunday). Free.

Wildseed Farms. US 290 east of Fredericskburg; (800) 848–0078; www.wildseedfarms.com. This attraction holds the record as the largest family-owned wildflower seed farm in the United States. There's a self-guided walking tour through the colorful grounds as well as a market center featuring all types of gift items. The farm is located 7 miles east of Fredericksburg on US 290. Open daily from 9:30 A.M. to 6:00 P.M. Free.

where to shop

Fredericksburg's many specialty shops offer antiques, linens, Texana, art, and collectibles. Most stores are housed in historic buildings along Main Street.

Charles Beckendorf Gallery. 150 North Adams Street; (800) 369–9004 or (830) 997–5955; www.beckendorf.com. This enormous gallery showcases the locally known work of artist Charles Beckendorf and is a good place to pick up a print of regional scenes, from one-room schoolhouses to brilliant fall scenes. Open daily.

where to eat

Altdorf German Biergarten and Restaurant. 301 West Main Street; (830) 997–7865. Take a break from shopping and enjoy some good German food in a pleasant outdoor setting. Sandwiches, steaks, burgers, and Mexican food are served here as well. There's also dining in an adjacent stone building erected by the city's pioneers. The restaurant is open for lunch and dinner daily; closed January. $–$$.

Peach Tree Tea Room. 210 South Adams Street; (830) 997–9527; www.peach-tree.com. Enjoy a lunch of quiche, soup, or salad in this tearoom, whose name is synonymous with Fredericksburg. Open for lunch Monday through Saturday. $.

where to stay

Fredericksburg is the capital city of Texas bed-and-breakfast inns, with accommodations in everything from Sunday houses to local farmhouses to residences just off Main Street. Several reservation services provide information on properties throughout the area.

Gastehaus Schmidt. 231 West Main Street; (866) 427–8374 or (830) 997–5612; www.fbg lodging.com. This service represents one hundred bed-and-breakfast accommodations, including cottages, log cabins, and a 125-year-old rock barn. All price ranges.

Be My Guest. 110 North Milam; (800) 364–8555 or (830) 997–7227; www.bemyguest fredericksburgtexas.com. More than twenty-five properties in Fredericksburg and nearby Lost Maples are handled by this service, with choices ranging from log cabins to historic homes. All price ranges.

Sunday House Inn and Suites. 501 East Main Street; (800) 274–3762 or (830) 997–4484; www.sundayhouseinnandsuites.com. Located on the eastern edge of town, this modern facility includes a restaurant, pool, and cable TV. $$–$$$.

Magnolia House. 101 East Hackberry; (800) 880–4374 or (830) 997–0306; www.magnolia -house.com. This historic bed-and-breakfast, constructed in 1923, offers guests a full breakfast. Only older children are permitted; call first. $$–$$$.

Peach Tree Inn and Suites. 401 South Washington; (800) 843–4666 or (830) 997–2117; www.thepeachtreeinn.com. This thirty-four-room inn offers guests a complimentary continental breakfast. Some rooms include refrigerators and microwaves. There's a playground for the kids and a pool as well. $–$$.

First Class Bed and Breakfast Reservation Service. 909 East Main Street; (888) 991–6749 or (830) 997–0443; www.fredericksburg-lodging.com. This service represents a wide variety of Fredericksburg area bed-and-breakfast properties and guest houses.

especially for winter texans

If you're traveling by RV or trailer, spend some time at the 113-site Lady Bird Johnson Municipal Park, just southwest of Fredericksburg on TX 16. Campsites have electrical, water, sewer, and cable TV hookups. There's a fourteen-day limit on camping from April through September. The park also has a self-guided nature trail. Pick up a checklist of birds or insects found in the region.

The park, located 3 miles south of Fredericksburg on TX 16 South, sports a nine-hole golf course, six tennis courts, and badminton and volleyball courts. There's also a seventeen-acre lake for fishing. For more information call (830) 997–4202.

enchanted rock state natural area

Whether you're a climber or just looking for a good picnic spot, drive out to Enchanted Rock State Natural Area (325–247–3903; www.tpwd.state.tx.us). Located 18 miles north of Fredericksburg on RR 965, this state park features the largest stone formation in the West. Nationally, this 640-acre granite outcropping takes second only to Georgia's Stone Mountain. According to Indian legend, the rock is haunted. Sometimes, as the rock cools at night, it makes a creaking sound, which probably accounts for the story.

People of all ages in reasonably good physical condition can enjoy a climb up Enchanted Rock. The walk takes about an hour, and hikers are rewarded with a magnificent view of the Hill Country. In warm weather (from April through October), start your ascent early in the morning before the relentless sun turns the rock into a griddle.

Experienced climbers can scale the smaller formations located adjacent to the main dome. These bare rocks are steep and dotted with boulders and crevices, and their ascent requires special equipment.

Picnic facilities and a sixty-site primitive campground at the base of the rock round out the offerings here. No vehicular camping is permitted. Buy all your supplies in Fredericksburg; there are no concessions here. To prevent overcrowding, a limited number of visitors are allowed in the park during peak periods. Arrive early. Open daily. Fee.

northeast

day trip 01

northeast

old-world fun:
new braunfels, gruene

new braunfels

If you're looking for a romantic getaway in a historic inn or a weekend of outdoor fun, New Braunfels is the place. Just half an hour northeast of San Antonio on I–35, this town of 36,000 offers something for every interest, from antiques and water sports to German culture.

In the 1840s, a group of German businessmen bought some land in Texas, planning to parcel off the acreage to German immigrants. Led by Prince Carl of Germany's Solms-Braunfels region, the group came to Texas to check on their new purchase. They discovered that it was more than 300 miles from the Texas coast, far from supplies in San Antonio, and located in the midst of Comanche Indian territory. Prince Carl sent a letter warning other settlers not to come, but it was too late—almost 400 already had set sail for Texas. The prince saved the day by buying another parcel of land, this one in the central part of the state. Called "The Fountains" by the Indians, it offered plentiful springs and agricultural opportunities. The Germans soon divided the land into farms, irrigating with springwater. The settlement they founded was named New Braunfels in honor of their homeland.

New Braunfels has never forgotten these ties to the old country. Even today German is spoken in many local homes. Every November the town puts on its lederhosen for Wurstfest, one of the largest German celebrations in the country. During these ten days, polka the night away, listen to well-known yodelers and accordionists, or dine on schnitzel at this family-friendly festival. The entire community of New Braunfels is filled with activities

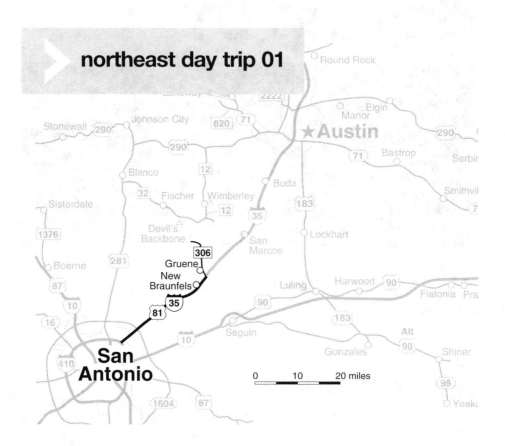

northeast day trip 01

during the Wurstfest weeks, with events that range from arts and crafts shows to boating regattas. The New Braunfels Conservation Society conducts several special tours of Conservation Plaza during weekends, touring restored German buildings including a general store, music studio, cabinet shop, and the Church Hill School.

The German settlers were a practical lot, and they saved old items of every description. Everything from handmade cradles to used bottles and jars were kept and passed down through generations. Because of this, New Braunfels touts itself as "the Antique Capital of Texas."

The early settlers of New Braunfels also were attracted by the Comal and Guadalupe Rivers. Today swimmers, rafters, inner-tubers, and campers are drawn to these shady banks. The 2-mile-long Comal holds the distinction as the world's shortest river. Its crystal-clear waters begin with the springs in downtown Landa Park, eventually merging with the Guadalupe River, home to many local outfitters. Located on the River Road scenic drive, the outfitters provide equipment and transportation for inner-tubers and rafters of all skill levels who like nothing better on a hot Texas day than to float down the cypress-shaded waters.

where to go

Chamber of Commerce. 390 South Seguin Avenue; (800) 572–2626; www.nbcham.org. Drop by for maps, brochures, shopping information, and friendly hometown advice about the area. Open daily.

Schlitterbahn Waterpark Resort New Braunfels. 305 West Austin Street; (830) 625–2351; www.schlitterbahn.com. From I–35 take the Boerne exit (Loop 337) to Common Street, then turn left and continue to Liberty Street. This water park ranks first in Texas and is tops in the United States among seasonal water parks. With sixty-five acres and 3 miles of tubing fun, this is the largest water theme park in the state.

Schlitterbahn, which means "slippery road" in German, is also the largest tubing park in the world, with nine tube chutes, two uphill water coasters, seventeen water slides, five playgrounds, and more. The Comal River supplies 24,000 gallons a minute of cool spring-water and also provides the only natural river rapids found in a water theme park.

Among the most colorful rides are the Soda Straws, huge Plexiglas-enclosed slides that take riders from the top of a 27-foot concrete soda glass to a pool below. In 1986 the glasses were filled with 2,000 gallons of soda and Blue Bell ice cream to create the world's largest Coke float. There's a steep 60-foot Schlittercoaster and the mile-long Raging River tube chute for daredevils and a 50,000-gallon hot tub with a swim-up bar and a gentle wave pool for the less adventurous.

Two popular attractions here are the Boogie Bahn, a moving mountain of water for surfing, and the Dragon Blaster, the world's first uphill water coaster. The latter shoots inner-tube riders uphill for a roller-coaster-type ride through hills, dips, and curves. Plan to spend a whole day here, and bring a picnic if you like. Open May through September. Fee.

Sophienburg Museum. 401 West Coll Street; (830) 629–1572. For a look at the hard-working people who settled this rugged area, spend an hour or two at the Sophienburg. Named for the wife of settlement leader Prince Carl, the museum displays a reproduction of an early New Braunfels home, a doctor's office (complete with medical tools), a blacksmith's shop, and carriages used by early residents, along with other exhibits. Open daily, but call for hours. Fee.

Lindheimer Home. 491 Comal Avenue; (830) 608–1512. Located on the banks of the Comal River, this home belonged to Ferdinand Lindheimer, a botanist who lent his name to more than thirty Texas plant species. Now restored, it contains early memorabilia from Lindheimer's career as both botanist and newspaper publisher. A backyard garden is filled with examples of his native flora discoveries. Hours are seasonal; call before you go. Fee.

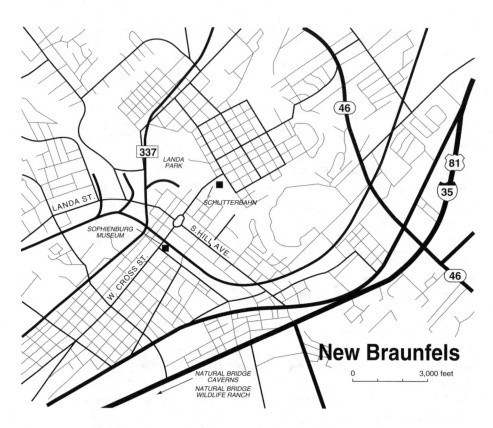

Museum of Texas Handmade Furniture. 1370 Church Hill Drive, in Conservation Plaza; (830) 629–6504. This nineteenth-century home contains cedar, oak, and cypress furniture handcrafted by early German settlers. Open Tuesday through Sunday from Memorial Day through Labor Day and on weekend afternoons the rest of the year. Fee.

Natural Bridge Caverns. On RR 3009, southwest of New Braunfels; (830) 651–6101; www.naturalbridgecaverns.com. Named for the rock arch over the entrance, this cave is one of the most spectacular in the area. The largest cave in central and southern Texas, it has wide, well-lit trails, perfect for introducing young visitors to the beauties of this under-ground world. Most visitors take the North Cavern Tour; tours depart at least every thirty minutes and last about seventy-five minutes. Tours take visitors through enormous rooms that look like the playing fields of prehistoric dinosaurs, rooms with names like the Castle of the White Giants. And for the most active members of your party, there's the South Cavern Tour, an adventure tour for which guests are outfitted in spelunking gear. The moderate-to-hard tour includes rappelling and crawling through passageways to view rarely seen cave features such as a 14-foot "soda straw," one of the largest such formations in North America. You'll need to make special reservations for this tour. Open daily year-round; phone for tour times. Fee.

> ## wurstfest
>
> *November's Wurstfest holds the title as one of the country's largest German cele-*
> *brations, an event filled with plenty of old-world atmosphere. At family-friendly*
> *Wurstfest, a salute to sausage (not to mention plenty of suds and song), you can*
> *polka the night away, listen to well-known yodelers and accordionists, or dine on*
> *schnitzel.*
>
> *The entire community of New Braunfels is filled with activities during the*
> *Wurstfest weeks, with events that range from arts and crafts shows to boating*
> *regattas and organized walks, runs, and bike rides.*

Natural Bridge Wildlife Ranch. Next to the caverns; (830) 438–7400; http://wildliferanch texas.com. From I–35 south of New Braunfels, take RR 3009 west. From TX 46 west of town, you can take a left on RR 1863 for a slightly longer but very scenic route.

For more than a century this property has operated as a family ranch, and since 1984 it has showcased exotic species, today holding the title as the oldest and most visited safari park in the state. More than fifty native, exotic, and endangered species roam the grounds. The ranch offers a drive past zebras, gazelles, antelopes, ostriches, and more. You'll be given animal feed when you arrive, so be prepared for the animals to come right up to the car for a treat. (And watch out, or the ostrich will put his head inside the car in search of that food!) A large cat run gives jaguars and cougars plenty of room to stroll, and another area houses three species of primates, scarlet macaws, and other exotic birds. A walking area holds some species that require a little more attention, such as reticulated giraffes, Bennett wallabies, and Patagonian cavies. Children love the petting zoo for the chance to get face to face with pint-size, friendly animals. Open daily. Fee.

Landa Park. Landa and San Antonio Streets; (830) 608–2160. Named for Joseph Landa, New Braunfels's first millionaire, this downtown park includes a miniature train, a glass-bottom boat cruise, a golf course, and a one-and-a-half-acre spring-fed swimming pool. This is the headwaters of the Comal River, where springs gush eight million gallons of pure water every hour. Picnicking is welcome in the park, but no camping. Free.

Canyon Lake. FM 306, northwest of town; (800) 528–2104. With 80 miles of protected shoreline, Canyon Lake is very popular with campers, cyclists, scuba divers, and boaters. The lake has seven parks with boat ramps and picnic facilities.

River Road. This winding drive stretches northwest of the city for 18 miles from Loop 337 at the city limits to the Canyon Lake Dam. It's lined with river outfitters and beautiful spots to pull over and look at the rapids, which delight rafters, canoeists, and inner-tubers.

Rockin' R River Rides. 1405 Gruene Road; (800) 55–FLOAT or (830) 629–9999; www.rockinr.com. You can take a river ride here anytime between March and October. Excursions range from family tubing trips to white-water thrillers. This company also operates a campground, Camp Hueco Springs, on River Road.

The Children's Museum. Off I–35 at exit 187; (830) 620–0939. Bring the kids to enjoy hands-on fun at this interactive museum that features a television studio. Open Tuesday through Sunday (Sunday afternoon only). Fee.

where to shop

New Braunfels Marketplace. Exits 187 and 189 off I–35; (830) 620–6806; www.nbmarket place.com. What started out as a single factory store has become a destination for busloads of shoppers from Houston and Dallas. Goods from sportswear to books to leather goods are featured in the many shops. Open daily.

where to eat

Oma's Haus. Take Seguin exit 189 off I–35 and drive east to 541 TX 46 South; (830) 625–3280. This restaurant serves a wide selection of German dishes in a family atmosphere. The menu includes chicken and pork schnitzel, and a specialty of the house called Oma's Pride, a spinach-filled pastry shell. For the less adventurous, chicken-fried steak and chicken breast also are offered. Open for lunch and dinner daily. $$.

Naegelin's Bakery. 129 South Seguin Avenue; (830) 625–5722. Naegelin's has operated on the same spot since 1868. The original building is gone now, replaced by the current structure in 1942. The store's specialty is apple strudel, a 2-foot-long creation that is certain to make any pastry lover's mouth water. During the holidays, some of Naegelin's best sellers are *springerle,* a licorice cookie, and *lebkucken,* a frosted gingerbread cookie. Open Monday through Saturday. $. No credit cards.

New Braunfels Smokehouse. TX 46 and US 81; (830) 625–2416; www.nbsmoke house.com. If you get the chance to attend Wurstfest, you'll undoubtedly sample the product of this smokehouse. For this fall event, New Braunfels Smokehouse produces between 40,000 and 60,000 pounds of sausage. That sausage is the specialty of the house, but the restaurant has a little of everything, including smoked ham and barbecued brisket. A large gift shop up front offers Texas specialty foods and cookbooks. The company's mail-order business ships more than 600,000 catalogs to sausage lovers around the country. Open daily. $–$$.

where to stay

New Braunfels has plenty of accommodations for everyone. Check with the chamber of commerce at (800) 572–2626.

Prince Solms Inn. 295 East San Antonio Street; (800) 625–9169 or (830) 625–9169; www.princesolmsinn.com. Built in 1900, this quiet bed-and-breakfast has two suites and a guest parlor downstairs; upstairs there are eight guest rooms. All rooms are furnished with period antiques. $$–$$$.

Faust Hotel. 240 South Seguin Avenue; (830) 625–7791; www.fausthotel.com. A New Braunfels tradition, this 1929 four-story, renovated hotel features a bar that's popular with locals and visitors. The lobby is appointed with beautiful antique furnishings. $$.

John Newcombe's Tennis Ranch. 325 Mission Valley Road; (800) 444–6204; www.newktennis.com. This resort is especially noted for its tennis facilities, with covered, clay, and lighted courts. Professional instruction is available, and during the summer the resort offers children's learning programs. $$–$$$.

especially for winter texans

Heidelberg Lodges. 1020 North Houston Avenue; (830) 625–9967. Located near the headwaters of the Comal River, this scenic family resort is popular in the summer with swimmers, snorkelers, and scuba divers. During the off-season it's home to Winter Texans, who are welcomed with potluck dinners and get-togethers. Accommodations include A-frame cottages and motel units. Call for long-term winter rates. $$.

gruene

Although it has the feel of a separate community, Gruene actually sits within the northern New Braunfels city limits. Exit I–35 on FM 306 and head west for 1½ miles to Hunter Road. Turn left and continue to Gruene. Like Waxahachie and Refugio, the pronunciation of Gruene is one of those things that sets a real Texan apart. To sound like a local, just say "Green" when referring to this weekend destination.

In the days when cotton was king, Gruene was a roaring town on the banks of the Guadalupe River. Started in the 1870s by H. D. Gruene, the community featured a swinging dance hall and a cotton gin. Prosperity reigned until the boll weevil came to Texas, with the Great Depression right on its heels. Gruene's foreman hanged himself from the water tower, and H. D.'s plans for the town withered like the cotton in the fields. Gruene became a ghost town.

One hundred years after its founding, investors began restoring Gruene's historic buildings, and little by little businesses began moving into the once-deserted structures. Now Gruene is favored by antiques shoppers, barbecue and country music lovers, and those looking to step back into a simpler time. On weekdays you may find Gruene's streets quiet, but expect crowds every weekend.

Gruene is compact, with everything within easy walking distance. If you'd like more information on the community's history, pick up a free copy of "A Pedestrian Guide for Gruene Guests" at local shops.

More than one hundred arts and crafts vendors sell their wares during Market Days. This event is held February through November on the third Saturday and Sunday of the month, and a Christmas market takes place on the first weekend in December. The event is juried, and artisans are carefully selected; all items sold are made by the vendors themselves.

where to go

Gruene Hall. 1281 Gruene Road; (830) 606–1281; www.gruenehall.com. The oldest dance hall in Texas is as lively today as it was a century ago. Dances and concerts are regularly held here (even though the hall still offers only natural air-conditioning), and it is also open to tour. Burlap bags draped from the ceiling dampen the sound, and 1930s advertisements decorate the walls. The hall opens at 11:00 A.M. most days. On weekdays, there's usually no cover charge for evening performances; weekend cover charges vary with the performer. Call for a schedule of events.

where to shop

Gruene General Store. 1610 Hunter Road; (830) 629–6021. This shop brings back memories of small-town life during Gruene's heyday as a cotton center. This was the first mercantile store, built in 1878 to serve the families that worked on the cotton farms. It also served as a stagecoach stop and a post office. Today, instead of farm implements and dry goods, this general store sells cookbooks, fudge, and Texas-themed clothing. Belly up for a soda from the old-fashioned fountain and have a taste of homemade fudge.

Gruene River Raft Company. 1404 Gruene Road; (888) 705–2800 or (830) 625–2800. See the Guadalupe at your own pace—during a leisurely inner-tube ride or on an exciting white-water raft journey—with this outfitter.

Lone Star Country Goods. 1613 Hunter Road; (830) 609–1613. Bring the cowboy look to your home with the accessories in this shop. Lamps, dinnerware, and folk art are offered for sale.

Texas Homegrown. 1641 Hunter Road; (830) 629–3176. Like the name suggests, the merchandise here is Texas-themed and features everything from bluebonnet earrings to coyote T-shirts. Open daily.

Gruene Antique Company. 1607 Hunter Road; (830) 629–7781. Built in 1904, this was once a mercantile store. Today it's divided into several vendor areas and filled with antiques. Open daily.

Buck Pottery. 1296 Gruene Road; (830) 629–7975. Here you can watch crafters make pottery in the back room. This shop sells dinnerware, gift items, and outdoor pots, all made with unleaded glazes. Open daily.

Gruene Haus Country Store. 1297 Gruene Road; (830) 620–7454. Built in the 1880s, this shop was the former home of H. D. Gruene's foreman. Linens, lace runners, silk bluebonnets, gifts for cat lovers, and decorative accessories are offered for sale. Open daily.

where to eat

Janie's Table. 1299 Gruene Road; (830) 629–6121. Outstanding barbecue, potato salad, and beans are popular choices at this restaurant (formerly Guadalupe Smoked Meats), housed in the old Martin Brothers Store. The owners also operate a mail-order business for people who can't find barbecue like this at home. Open daily for lunch and dinner. $$.

Gristmill Restaurant and Bar. 1287 Gruene Road; (830) 625–0684; www.gristmill restaurant.com. Housed in the ruins of a century-old cotton gin, this restaurant serves chicken, chicken-fried steak, catfish, burgers, and other Texas favorites. You can eat inside or outside on the deck overlooking the Guadalupe River. Open daily. $$.

where to stay

Gruene Mansion Inn. 1275 Gruene Road; (830) 629–2641; www.gruenemansioninn.com. Guests at this inn stay in restored 1870s cottages on a bluff overlooking the Guadalupe River. Eight lovely rooms are decorated with period antiques. A two-night rental is required on weekends. $$$. No credit cards.

day trip 02

northeast

shop 'til you drop:
san marcos, buda

san marcos

San Marcos is located 51 miles northeast of San Antonio on I–35, a drive that's always crowded, especially on Friday and Sunday afternoons. Like neighboring New Braunfels, San Marcos is best known for its pure spring waters. The San Marcos River, which has been used by humans for more than 13,000 years, flows through town, providing the city with beautiful swimming and snorkeling spots and a family educational park.

Permanent settlement of the area began in 1845. Today San Marcos is a popular tourist town and the home of Texas State University (formerly Southwest Texas State University).

This community is a shopping stop for many travelers. San Marcos is home to the largest outlet malls in Texas, ones that bring devoted shoppers by the busload from as far as Dallas, Houston, and Mexico. In fact, the malls rank as one of the top tourist attractions in Texas!

These mega-shopping stops are located alongside I–35 at exit 200. Whether you're in search of clothing or china, children's toys or summer luggage, you'll find it at these Texas-size malls.

where to go

Tourist Information Center. Exit 204B (C. M. Allen Parkway) from I–35 on the northwest side of town; (888) 200–5620 or (512) 353–3435. Stop here for brochures on area attractions and accommodations, as well as free maps. Open daily. Free.

Aquarena Center. 921 Aquarena Springs Drive; (800) 999–9767 or (512) 245–7570; www .aquarena.txstate.edu. Take Aquarena Springs exit from I–35 and follow signs west of the highway. This resort dates from 1928, when A. B. Rogers purchased 125 acres at the headwaters of the San Marcos River to create a grand hotel. He added glass-bottom boats to cruise Spring Lake, fed by more than 200 springs that produce 150 million gallons daily. Pristine artesian water is home to many fish (including some white albino catfish) and various types of plant life. Today visitors can still enjoy a cruise on the glass-bottom boats and see the site of an underwater archaeological dig that unearthed the remains of Clovis Man, one of the hunter-gatherers who lived on the San Marcos River more than 13,000 years ago.

Formerly a family amusement park, today Aquarena Center, operated by Texas State University, focuses on ecotourism, with exhibits and activities aimed at introducing visitors

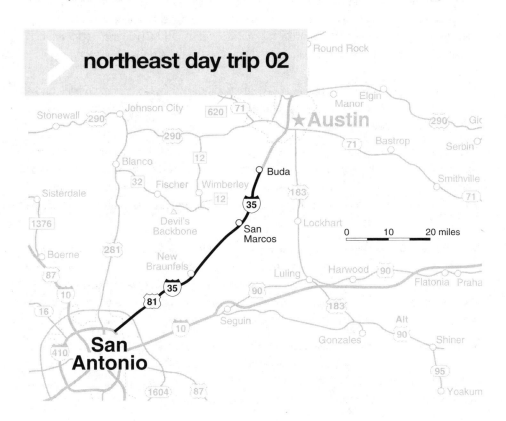

northeast day trip 02

of all ages to the natural history and natural attractions of this region. This family park features glass-bottom boat rides, an endangered-species exhibit, the San Xavier Spanish Mission, an 1890s general store, historic homes from San Marcos's earliest days, and plenty of educational fun. The park offers special guided trips that feature the historic attractions as well as other excursions focusing on endangered species, archaeological sites, birdwatching, and the flora and fauna of the area.

Open daily, although hours change seasonally. Fee.

Wonder World. Exit at Wonder World Drive on the south side of San Marcos and follow signs for about a mile; (877) 492–4657, or (512) 392–3760 for group and tour reservations; www.wonderworldpark.com. A guided tour lasting nearly two hours covers the entire park, including the seven-and-a-half-acre Texas Wildlife Park, Texas's largest petting zoo. A miniature train chugs through the animal enclosure, stopping to allow riders to pet and feed white-tailed deer, wild turkeys, and many exotic species.

The next stop on the tour is Wonder Cave, created during a three-and-a-half-minute earthquake thirty million years ago. The same earthquake produced the Balcones Fault, an 1,800-mile line separating the western Hill Country from the flat eastern farmland. Within the cave is the actual crack in the two land masses, with huge boulders lodged in the fissure. At the end of the cave tour, take the elevator ride to the top of the 110-foot Tejas Tower, which offers a spectacular view of the Balcones Fault and the contrasting terrain it produced.

The last stop is the Anti-Gravity House, a structure employing optical illusions and a slanted floor to create the feeling that you're leaning backward. In this house, water appears to run uphill, yet another illusion. Fee.

City Park. Across from Texas State University. Concessioners here rent inner tubes so that you can float down the San Marcos Loop. The floating excursion, in seventy-two-degree water, takes about an hour and a half. Snorkeling is popular here as well, and you might see a freshwater prawn (which can reach 12 inches in length), the rare San Marcos salamander, or one of fifty-two kinds of fish.

Millie Seaton Collection of Dolls and Toys. 1104 West Hopkins; (512) 396–1944; www .millies-dolls.com. For more than thirty years, Millie Seaton has collected dolls from around the world. The number of dolls grew and grew—until finally the avid collector bought a three-story Victorian home just to house the 8,000 dolls! Call to set up a time with Millie or one of her docents for a guided walk through this cherished collection. Donation appreciated.

John J. Stokes San Marcos River Park. From TX 80, turn right on River Road for about 1 mile; turn left on County Road to the island; (512) 393–8404. Operated by the city of San Marcos, this day-use park is also known as Thompson's Island and is located across the river from the A. E. Wood State Fish Hatchery. The park offers river access but no facilities. Fee.

Calaboose Museum of African American History. Martin Luther King Drive and Fredericksburg Street; (512) 393–8421. Housed in the 1873 building that served as Hays County's first jail, this museum preserves the history of the African Americans of San Antonio, starting in the nineteenth century. Along with an extensive collection of books and artifacts, the museum also schedules frequent educational programs and public events. Open by appointment. Fee.

Living History Trolley Tour. Tanger Outlet Center Visitor Center, exit 200 from I–35 south of San Marcos; (512) 396–3739. These guided tours are scheduled for 2:00 P.M. on the first Saturday of each month, departing from the Tanger Outlet Center Visitor Center. The trolley tours include stops at sites featured in the novels *True Women* and *Hill Country,* as well as the Courthouse Square, the San Marcos River, Aquarena Springs, and historic mansions. Reservations required. Fee.

Driving Tour of Old San Marcos. The Heritage Association of San Marcos designed this self-drive tour of Old San Marcos, including the Courthouse Square, historic homes, and the Belvin Street National Register District, filled with Victorian homes. For a free copy of the driving tour, contact the convention and visitors bureau or see www.centuryinter .net/smheritage.

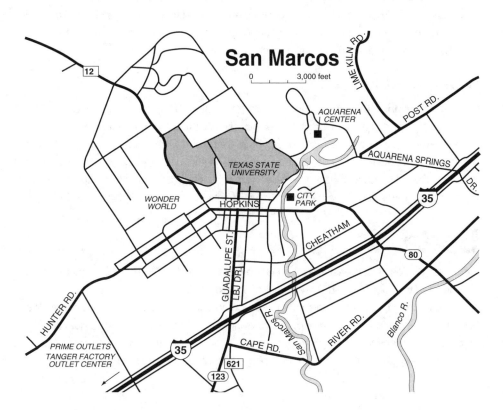

Central Texas Wing of the Confederate Air Force. 1841 Airport Drive; (512) 396–1943. Housed in a vintage wooden hangar at the San Marcos Municipal Airport, this collection contains World War II artifacts and several historic aircraft. A unique display is a replica of a torpedo bomber plane, the CAF Japanese Kate, built for the movie *Tora, Tora, Tora*. Open Monday, Wednesday, Friday, and Saturday from 9:00 A.M. to 4:00 P.M. Donation appreciated.

where to shop

Prime Outlets. Exit 200 from I–35 on the south side of San Marcos; (800) 628–9465 or (512) 396–2200; www.primeoutlets.com. This open-air mall features more than one hundred shops that sell direct from the factory. Luggage, shoes, leather goods, outdoor gear, china, kitchen goods, and other specialties are offered for sale. Chartered buses from as far as Dallas and Houston stop here regularly. Open daily.

Tanger Factory Outlet Center. Exit 200 from I–35 south of San Marcos; (800) 408–8424; www.tangeroutlet.com. More than thirty shops feature name-brand designers and manufacturers in this open-air mall. Housewares, footwear, home furnishings, leather goods, perfumes, and books are offered. Open daily.

Centerpoint Station. Exit 200 from I–35 south of San Marcos; (512) 392–1103; www.center pointstation.com. This charming shop, built like an old-fashioned general store, is filled with Texas and country collectibles, T-shirts, gourmet gift foods, cookbooks, and more. Up front, a counter serves sandwiches, malts, and ice cream.

where to stay

Crystal River Inn. 326 West Hopkins Street; (888) 396–3739 or (512) 396–3739; www.crystalriverinn.com. The Crystal River Inn offers visitors elegant Victorian accommodations in rooms named for Texas rivers. Owners Cathy and Mike Dillon provide guests with a selection of special packages, including tubing on the San Marcos, sunset cruises at Aquarena Springs, and a popular weekend murder mystery, where costumed guests work to solve a mystery using clues based on actual events in San Marcos history. $$–$$$.

buda

From San Marcos, it's an easy fifteen-minute drive north on I–35 to Buda, a former railroad town located on Loop 4 (Main Street) west of the highway.

Buda is one of the most mispronounced communities in Texas (and with names like Gruene, Leakey, and Boerne around, that's saying a lot). To sound like a local, just say "b-YOU-da." The name has caused more than one foreign visitor to come here expecting an old-world Hungarian settlement. Though possibly a reference to Budapest, the name is more likely of Spanish origin. According to legend, several widows cooked in the local hotel restaurant that was popular with employees of the International–Great Northern Railroad. The Spanish word for "widow" is *viuda*. Since the *v* is pronounced as a *b* in Spanish, Buda may be a phonetic spelling for *viuda*.

Buda is still a railroad town, with double tracks running parallel to Main Street.

where to shop

Many Buda stores are closed Monday through Wednesday, although some are open by appointment. Most shops are located in a 2-block stretch of Main Street.

Texas Hatters. Exit 220 on east side of I–35; (512) 295–4287; www.texashatters.com. This store's founder, the late Manny Gammage, was "Texas's Hatmaker to the Stars." His hats topped the heads of Roy Rogers, Willie Nelson, Ronald Reagan, Burt Reynolds, and many other celebrities whose pictures decorate the shop walls. Besides the obligatory cowboy hats, this store also sells hand-blocked high-rollers, Panamas, and derbies. Open Tuesday through Saturday.

alice's restaurant

There's not a lot in Niederwald these days. Come to think of it, there never has been a lot in Niederwald. Founded by German pioneers and named "brushwood" for the mesquite that dots the area, the town was a stop on the old Austin–San Antonio road. Now it's still a stop on today's Austin–San Antonio road, I–35.

But there's one good reason to make a day-trip detour to Niederwald: Alice's Restaurant. This eatery, housed in a frame house and accompanied by a small biergarten, combines good food and good music in one entree, with a healthy side serving of Austin funkiness. The menu ranges from pork chops to shrimp skewers, but as much a draw is the live music. Austin talent, including many singer-songwriters, headline here three nights a week.

To reach Alice's Restaurant, in Buda turn east off I–35 on FM 2001 (exit 220) and continue 9 miles to the intersection of TX 21. Alice's is just a quarter mile east of the intersection on TX 21 at 14100 Camino Real. (If you'd prefer to take this detour from San Marcos, continue on this day trip, then head east on TX 21 in San Marcos for 14 miles.) For a schedule of performers, call (512) 376–2782 or see www.alicesrestauranttx.com. Alice's is open Thursday from 10:00 A.M. to 10:00 P.M., Friday and Saturday 10:00 A.M. until midnight, and Sunday from 11:00 A.M. to 3:00 P.M.

day trip 03

northeast

capital fun:
austin

austin

Maybe it's the college student population that tops 50,000. Maybe it's the live music industry that has made this city a haven for fans and performers alike. Or maybe it's just geography, with the city situated on a downtown lake and perched at the edge of a rambling Hill Country lake that offers everything from windsurfing to nude sunbathing.

Whatever the reason, there's one thing for certain: Austin is a town that doesn't want to grow up. Like a perpetual teenager, the capital of Texas is brash, sassy, and sometimes just downright silly. Sure, the city is home to both high-tech industry and countless state officials, but residents use any excuse to toss off the ties and three-piece suits. They don elaborate costumes for an annual party in Pease Park to celebrate (believe it or not) the birthday of Eeyore, the pal of Winnie the Pooh. But those costumes are just a dress rehearsal for the Halloween party that takes place on Sixth Street, complete with 20,000 to 70,000 merrymakers.

Austin began in 1835 as a small village named Waterloo, settled by Jacob Harrell along the banks of Waller, Shoal, and Barton Creeks, tributaries of the Colorado River. At the time, the territory was the home of the Comanche and Tonkawa Indians and fell under the governance of Mexico.

As Harrell constructed a stockade for protection of the new settlement, the Texas War of Independence was under way. The next year, the Republic of Texas declared its independence from Mexico. Harrell's friend, Mirabeau B. Lamar, became vice president of the new nation and soon visited Waterloo on a buffalo hunt. The beauty and natural resources of Waterloo impressed Lamar.

Months after his visit, Lamar succeeded war hero Gen. Sam Houston as president of the republic. As one of Lamar's first acts, Waterloo became the capital city, and its name was changed to Austin in honor of Stephen F. Austin, one of the first colonizers of Texas. The new capital did not meet the approval of Sam Houston, who thought the city was too close to Mexico and too far from the Gulf Coast to serve as the seat of the young nation's government.

The constant threat of attack by both Indians and Mexican troops caused concern in the new capital throughout Lamar's term of office. When Sam Houston was again elected president of the republic in 1841, he decided the government should be relocated to the security of his namesake city, Houston, and sent the Texas Rangers to obtain the state's papers.

northeast day trip 03

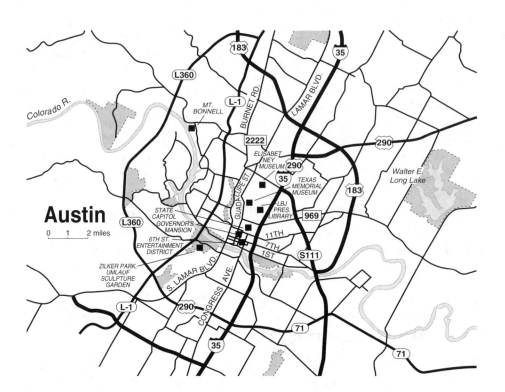

The residents of Austin quickly worked to stop the action in a move called the Archive Wars. The citizens captured the papers from the Texas Rangers and returned them to Austin, although for the next several years the government operated out of Houston. Finally, statewide referendums in 1850 and 1872 settled the matter. Austin eventually became the seat of government for the state as Texas joined the Union in 1845.

Austin experienced steady growth, and in 1871 the railroad came to town. Soon the railroad hauled granite blocks from the western Hill Country community of Marble Falls to downtown Austin to construct a new state capitol, dedicated in 1888.

For years, the city was plagued by flooding along the Colorado River. In 1938 the Lower Colorado River Authority began constructing a series of dams along the Texas length of the Colorado River, forming the chain of Highland Lakes including Austin's Town Lake and Lake Austin.

Lake Austin begins at the foot of the Hill Country and flows for 22 miles through the western part of the city. Although high-priced residential structures are scattered along the shores, much of the countryside is still preserved in public parks. Lake Austin empties into Town Lake, a narrow stretch of water that slices through the center of downtown. Beautifully planted greenbelts compose the shoreline, which includes 15 miles of hike and bike trails. Although swimming and motorboating are prohibited, visitors can rent canoes near the lakeside Hyatt Regency Austin Hotel. The calm waters of Town Lake draw collegiate rowing teams from around the country to train in the warm climate.

Attractions abound on both sides of the Colorado River, most just a few minutes off I-35. A bit north of the river and within five minutes of the interstate are the best two shows in town: the Texas Legislature and the University of Texas. The legislature meets in the State Capitol from January through May in odd-numbered years. Even when this body is not in session, you can take a free tour of the historic building and watch the hustle and bustle of state government.

Parking at the capitol and downtown area comes at a premium. The best way to explore is aboard a 'Dillo, the free trolley service. Several different routes serve the downtown area. Of special interest to visitors is the "Tour the Town" 'Dillo (Route 470), which offers special service on weekends with stops at the LBJ Library, Zilker Park, and Congress Avenue. Night owls checking out the action along Sixth Street can hop the Starlight 'Dillo or the Moonlight 'Dillo as each access the entertainment district.

From the capitol, it's a ten-minute walk north on Congress Avenue to Martin Luther King Boulevard and the southern edge of the University of Texas campus. This sprawling institution boasts students and faculty from around the world and some of the finest educational facilities in the country. The centerpiece of the university is the Main Tower, illuminated by orange lights whenever the University of Texas Longhorns win. The tower stands in the open mall, which includes the large Student Union building where students and the general public can grab a low-priced lunch.

Guadalupe (pronounced in Austin as "GWAD-a-loop") Street divides the educational campus from a commercial strip called the Drag, the stretch of Guadalupe that runs from Martin Luther King Boulevard to Twenty-sixth Street. The area is always crowded and fun, filled with shops and eateries that cater to every student need. The People's Renaissance Market, just across the street from the Student Union, is an open-air bazaar where crafters sell their wares. It's especially popular with Austinites for Christmas shopping.

Most of the University of Texas grounds are closed to motorized traffic, but you can park at the LBJ Presidential Library and Museum, located on the north side of campus. Before touring the Presidential Library, walk to the fountain for an unparalleled view of both the university and downtown Austin.

As your day draws to a close, head back to Town Lake. During summer months, people flock to the shoreline near the Congress Avenue Bridge at Town Lake to witness the nightly departure of Mexican free-tailed bats from the Bat Colony. Austin boasts the largest urban population of bats in the nation.

Finally, spend your evening on Sixth Street, Austin's entertainment district that runs from Congress Avenue east to I-35. It's lined with restaurants, bars, and clubs featuring nightly music performed by Austin musicians. Friday and Saturday evenings are crowded. Be forewarned: Many clubs don't crank up the music until the wee hours.

where to go

Visitor Information Center. 201 East Second Street; (512) 478–0098. Stop here for attractions, trolley and bus routes, and dining information. Open daily and Sunday after-noons. Free.

Bob Bullock History Museum. North Congress Avenue and Martin Luther King Boulevard; (888) 369–7108 or (512) 936–8746; www.TheStoryofTexas.com. A favorite stop with visitors to the nearby State Capitol, this expansive museum includes three floors of Texas-related exhibits and audiovisual shows. The museum offers many interactive exhibits on the history of Texas as well as an IMAX theater. Open daily. Fee.

Bat Colony. Congress Avenue Bridge at Town Lake; (512) 478–0098. Austin is well known as home of its seasonal visitors: one-and-a-half million Mexican free-tailed bats that reside under the Congress Avenue Bridge during the summer months. Crowds gather along the banks of Town Lake every night at sundown to watch the bats leave their perch to feast upon the insects of the Hill Country. The best viewing is from the hike and bike trail, the bridge, or a free bat viewing area in the parking lot of the *Austin American-Statesman* at 305 South Congress Avenue. The peak spectator months are July and August. For more on the bats, check out the information kiosks at the Four Seasons Hotel at 98 San Jacinto Boulevard and the *Austin American-Statesman* parking lot on the south shore. Free.

Wild Basin Wilderness Preserve. 805 North Loop 360; (512) 327–7622. This 220-acre preserve offers a good look at the natural side of the Hill Country. More than 2 miles of trails wind through the brush; there's also an easy access trail. Open daily. Fee.

State Capitol. Eleventh Street and Congress Avenue; (512) 463–0063. You might think that Texas's motto is "The bigger, the better," especially after a visit to the State Capitol. Taller than its national counterpart, the pink granite building houses the governor's office, the Texas Legislature, and several other executive state agencies. Guided tours depart from the visitor complex every thirty minutes. Free.

Capitol Complex Visitor Center. East Eleventh and Brazos; (512) 305–8400. Learn more about the capitol complex in this visitor center and museum housed in the 1857 General Land Office, the oldest government office building in the state. Once the workplace of short-story writer O. Henry, this building is now filled with exhibits and displays to introduce visitors to the workings of state government. The center, which is located on the southeast corner of the capitol grounds, also includes a Texas Travel Center with information about statewide travel. Open daily 9:00 A.M.–5:00 P.M. Free.

Governor's Mansion. 1010 Colorado Street; (512) 463–5516; www.txfgm.org/visitor.html. For more than 130 years, Texas governors have enjoyed the opulence of this grand home. Visitors are taken past the main staircase, through the formal parlor, and finally into the dining room. Tours (scheduled every twenty minutes) are conducted Monday through Thursday from 10:00 A.M. to noon. Call to check the status of tours; the home is sometimes closed because of incoming dignitaries. Free.

Lyndon Baines Johnson Presidential Library. 2313 Red River Street; (512) 721–0200; www.lbjlib.utexas.edu. (From I–35, exit west at Twenty-sixth Street.) Located on the campus of the University of Texas, this facility serves as a reminder of the Hill Country's most famous resident, Lyndon Baines Johnson. The library is filled with more than thirty-five million historic documents, housed in archival boxes and available for scholarly research. The first two floors offer films on Johnson's life and career, as well as exhibits featuring jeweled gifts from foreign dignitaries and simpler handmade tokens from appreciative Americans. Visitors also can take in special displays of political, civil rights, and educational memorabilia. The top floor holds a reproduction of LBJ's Oval Office, furnished as it was during his term. Open daily. Free.

Austin Children's Museum. 201 Colorado Street; (512) 472–2499; www.austinkids.org. The museum has operated in Austin since 1983 but in 1997 moved to the 19,000-square-foot Dell Discovery Center, named for Austin computer mogul Michael Dell. Hands-on activities for educational fun fill the dynamic, multilevel facility. Infants and toddlers crawl through a Hill Country landscape, while older visitors measure wind speed, slide down a time tower, or experiment with audio technology in a sound studio. Fee.

Zilker Park. (512) 472–4914. From I–35, take the Riverside Drive exit west and continue to Barton Springs Road. Follow Barton Springs Road to the park. Located just south of Town Lake, this city park is a favorite with joggers, picnickers, swimmers, soccer teams, and kite flyers. One of almost 200 parks in Austin, Zilker is the largest and most popular of the well-used facilities. The park was originally the site of temporary Franciscan missions in 1730 and was later used as a gathering place by Native Americans.

Here lies the beautiful spring-fed Barton Springs Pool, where you can take a dip in the sixty-eight-degree, crystal-clear waters all year. The park is also home to the Zilker Botanical Garden, which includes the Oriental Garden, a meditation trail, and the Rose Garden, as well as a Swedish log cabin dating from the 1840s. A Xeriscape Demonstration Garden displays more than fifty native and low-water-use trees, shrubs, groundcovers, and wildflowers resistant to Central Texas's hot summers. Nearby, the Cactus and Succulent Garden features mostly native West Texas cactus and succulents.

The Isamu Taniguchi Oriental Garden is highlighted by blooming cherry trees from mid-March through mid-April, followed by blossoming water lilies into the fall months. The Mabel Davis Rose Garden features beds ranging from the latest All-America Rose Society award winners to the antique shrub roses of the Republic of Texas collection. Peak blooming times are April to June and October.

The Herb and Fragrance Garden contains dozens of culinary and fragrant plants among the raised beds. The Hamilton Parr Memorial Azalea Garden, in bloom during March and April, contains dazzling azalea beds surrounding a shaded flagstone patio. Finally, the Douglas Blachly Butterfly Trail showcases local flowers and plants that attract numerous species of Texas butterflies. Visitors can view Austin's attractive butterflies and migrating species as well.

Things to see include a miniature train for the kids, dinosaur tracks, and a nature center. Free; fee for pool and train.

Town Lake Cruises. Depart from the dock of the Hyatt Regency Hotel at 208 Barton Springs Road; (512) 327–1388. Enjoy a ninety-minute excursion on Town Lake aboard the *Lone Star Riverboat* paddle wheeler. Public cruises March through late October; call for schedule. Fee.

Umlauf Sculpture Garden and Museum. 605 Robert E. Lee Road; (512) 445–5582; www.umlaufsculpture.org. Take a peaceful walk through this garden, featuring the works of Charles Umlauf, former professor emeritus at the University of Texas. Located off Barton Springs Road, near Zilker Park, the garden displays about sixty sculptures, and the museum exhibits about an equal number of smaller pieces. A video provides a look at the life of the sculptor. Open Wednesday through Sunday. Fee.

Elisabet Ney Museum. 304 East Forty-fourth Street; (512) 458–2255; www.ci.austin .tx.us/elisabetney. German immigrant Elisabet Ney was considered Texas's first sculptress, and this stone building served as her studio and home. It's filled with her statues, working drawings, and personal belongings. Ney's work also can be seen in the entrance of the State Capitol. Open Wednesday through Sunday. Free.

Austin Museum of Art Downtown. 823 Congress Avenue; (512) 495–9224; www .amoa.org. This downtown facility, a sister of the original museum at Laguna Gloria, features rotating exhibits. Open Tuesday through Saturday. Fee.

Austin Museum of Art at Laguna Gloria. 3809 West Thirty-fifth Street; (512) 458–8191; www.amoa.org. This Mediterranean-style villa, located on Lake Austin, was built in 1916. Today the elegant structure is home to a museum that hosts changing exhibits of twentieth-century art. Open Tuesday through Sunday. Fee; free on Thursday.

Lady Bird Johnson Wildflower Center. 4801 LaCrosse Avenue; (512) 292–4100; www.wildflower.org. (Take Loop 1 south ⁹⁄₁₀ mile south of Slaughter Lane.) This unique institution is the only one in the nation devoted to the conservation and promotion of native plants and flowers. The center was the dream of Lady Bird Johnson, wife of the late president. Mrs. Johnson was also responsible for the beautiful bluebonnet and wildflower plantings along the interstate highways in Texas.

The center, located on a 279-acre site in an $8 million facility, includes a children's discovery room, gallery, gift shop, and the Wildflower Cafe. Visitors can take a self-guided educational tour of the grounds; groups of ten or more may arrange for a guide. The center acts as an information clearinghouse, distributing numerous fact sheets on more than one hundred native species. Annual events include landscaping seminars and workshops. The center is open Tuesday through Sunday. Fee.

Jourdan-Bachman Pioneer Farm. East of town at 11418 Sprinkle Cut-Off Road; (512) 837–1215. Here children can watch daily chores of the period being carried out with authentic tools. The farm hosts special events such as A Taste of Texas Past, with old-time cooking methods and recipes. Hours vary seasonally. Fee.

Austin Nature and Science Center. 301 Nature Center Drive west of Zilker Park; (512) 327–8181; www.ci.austin.tx.us/ansc. The Hill Country's smallest residents, from field mice to raccoons, are featured at this popular ecological stop. All animals here have been injured and can no longer live in the wild. Along with exhibits on local wildlife, the center sponsors special workshops and festivities such as Hummingbird Day and Safari Day. Open daily. Free.

Texas Memorial Museum. 2400 Trinity Street; (512) 471–1604; www.texasmemorial museum.org. This university museum has exhibits on everything Texan, from dinosaur bones found in the Lone Star State to historic displays on the Indians who lived on this land. Open daily. Free.

Blanton Museum of Art. Southeast corner of Martin Luther King Boulevard and Congress Avenue, on the southern edge of the University of Texas campus; (512) 471–7324; www.blantonmuseum.org. This relocated museum opened in its new setting in spring 2006. The new facility includes a gallery building with an adjoining public plaza as well as the Education and Visitor Pavilion, scheduled to open in early 2007. The museum's collection includes more than 17,000 works and is recognized for its Old Master paintings, as well as modern and contemporary American and Latin American art. Fee.

Treaty Oak. 503 Baylor Street. This 600-year-old oak captured the nation's attention in 1989 when it was poisoned. It was once called the finest example of a tree in North America. Today one-third of the original tree is gone.

Hike and Bike Trails. Few metropolitan areas boast more fitness-conscious folks than Austin. Residents and visitors alike enjoy more than 25 miles of trails, including many around Town Lake. Pick up a free trail guide at the Parks and Recreation Department, 200 South Lamar Boulevard (512–974–6700).

Sixth Street. This entertainment district is one of the first introductions many visitors get to Austin, but it's just as popular with residents. Friday and Saturday nights are often standing room only in an entertainment district that's sometimes compared to New Orleans's Bourbon Street. Here blues rather than jazz is king, and it's found in little clubs such as Joe's Generic Bar, Maggie Mae's, and the 311 Club. They're all well received by music fans in this city that gave Janis Joplin her start years ago, as well as favorites such as Willie Nelson, Stevie Ray Vaughn, and the Fabulous Thunderbirds.

Austin Zoo. 10807 Rawhide Trail; (800) 291–1490 or (512) 288–1490; www.austinzoo .com. Bring along the kids to this privately owned zoo, located near Oak Hill, to enjoy pony rides, train rides, a petting zoo, and plenty of exotic creatures. Young visitors can purchase animal food to feed some of the inhabitants by hand. Open daily. Fee.

Mount Bonnell. 3800 Mount Bonnell Road. Climb up for a look across Lake Austin and the outlying Hill Country from atop one of the city's best lookouts. The view is located 1 mile past the west end of West Thirty-fifth Street. Closes at 10:00 P.M. daily. Free.

French Legation Museum. 802 San Marcos Street; (512) 472–8180; www.frenchlegation museum.org. Located in East Austin a few blocks from I–35, this unique museum is Austin's oldest remaining building. Its chief interest, however, lies in its role as the former French Legation during the years when Texas was an independent republic. Behind the home stands the only authentic reproduction of an early Creole kitchen. Open Tuesday through Sunday. Fee.

McKinney Falls State Park. Seven miles southeast of Austin on US 183; (512) 243–1643; www.tpwd.state.tx.us. This easily accessible state park is home to some low waterfalls that make this a favorite summertime getaway. The park also includes picnic facilities. Open daily. Fee.

O. Henry Home and Museum. 409 East Fifth Street; (512) 472–1903; www.ci.austin .tx.us/ohenry.htm. The short-story writer O. Henry (aka William Sidney Porter) lived in Austin for several years and resided in this small home. Today the author's belongings are on display in furnished rooms. Open Wednesday through Sunday. Free.

Texas State Library. 1201 Brazos Street; (512) 463–5480; www.tsl.state.tx.us. Located in the Lorenzo de Zavala Archives and Library Building just east of the State Capitol, this library contains both the state archives and the genealogical records of Texas. Open weekdays; geneaological library open Tuesday through Sunday. Free.

Harry Ransom Humanities Research Center. Guadalupe and Twenty-first Streets; (512) 471–8944; www.hrc.utexas.edu. Located on the University of Texas campus, this research center is noted for its copy of the Gutenburg Bible, one of only forty-eight known to exist. The center also houses a collection of photographic and film materials, including the world's first photograph. Open daily. Free.

where to shop

Callahan's General Store. 501 US 183; (512) 385–3452. Like a true general store, this sprawling store has just about everything a person could want. Western wear, saddles, boots, household items, and, yes, even chicks and ducks make up the extensive inventory. Open Monday through Saturday.

Bookpeople. 603 North Lamar Boulevard; (512) 472–5050. This megastore calls itself the largest bookstore in the United States, spanning four floors with more than 300,000 titles, 2,000 magazines and newspapers, and plenty of space just to hang out and browse. An espresso bar fills the first floor with the scent of fresh brew. Open daily.

Central Market. 4001 North Lamar Boulevard; (512) 206–1000. More than just a grocery store, this market is an international smorgasbord of produce, wines, meats, fish, and seasonings from around the globe. Regularly scheduled cooking classes offer visitors the chance to learn techniques from the pros. Open daily.

Clarksville Pottery. 4001 North Lamar Boulevard; (512) 454–9079. Shop for handmade stoneware from bowls and goblets to decorative ware at this fine crafts gallery. Another location in the Arboretum Market is convenient for shoppers in northwest Austin. Open daily.

Kerbey Lane and Jefferson Square. West Thirty-fifth Street at Kerbey Lane. This shopping enclave is a favorite for those looking for unique gift items, collectibles, and fashions. Located off Austin's medical district, the shops line Kerbey Lane and the open-air Jefferson Square center. Most shops open Monday through Saturday.

Renaissance Market. Twenty-third and Guadalupe Streets; no phone. Tucked right off the Drag in the University of Texas area, this open-air market is filled with the work of Austin artisans who sell handmade jewelry, woodcrafts, tie-dye shirts, glasswork, toys, pottery, and more one-of-a-kind items. This market claims to be Texas's only continuously operating open-air arts and crafts market. The number of artists varies by season, reaching a crescendo in the weeks before the holidays and a low point during the Christmas break, when UT students are few and far between. Open daily.

live music capital of the world

Austin has earned its nickname thanks to the large number of live music venues scattered throughout the city. On any given night, about one hundred venues ranging from concert halls to alternative bars to honky-tonks move to the sound of live music. The city has drawn many well-known names, who select Austin not just for performances but for their home. Today Austin is home to the Dixie Chicks, Shawn Colvin, Willie Nelson, Asleep at the Wheel, Don Walser, and others.

South Congress Avenue. Austin's best imports, antiques, and funky purchases can be acquired on South Congress Avenue, just south of Town Lake. This eclectic district is definitely for those looking for something a little different, whether that means a mariachi costume or wood carvings, hand-carved furniture or 1970s disco polyester getups. Most shops open Monday through Saturday and Sunday afternoons.

where to eat

Austin is filled with restaurants of every description, ranging from vegetarian to Vietnamese. For a list of Austin eateries, stop by the Austin Visitor Center at 300 Bouldin Avenue, located between Palmer Auditorium and City Auditorium. The center is open seven days a week.

Sixth Street has many restaurants and bars featuring live music, especially blues. Most of the dining establishments are casual.

Trudy's Texas Star. 409 West Thirtieth Street; (512) 477–2935. This popular university-area restaurant feeds you Tex-Mex for breakfast, lunch, and dinner. The green chicken (meaning the sauce, not the chicken) enchiladas are the best in town. Open daily. $–$$.

Iron Works Barbecue. 100 Red River Street; (512) 478–4855. This former foundry is still decorated with branding irons. Diners flock here to enjoy plates of juicy barbecue. If you have a big appetite, order the ribs. Open weekdays for lunch and dinner; lunch only on Saturday. $–$$.

Threadgill's. 6416 North Lamar Boulevard; (512) 451–5440; www.threadgills.com. Janis Joplin used to sing in this restaurant back in the early '60s. Today the place is best known for its home-style cooking, including jumbo chicken-fried steaks, fried chicken, and vegetables like Grandma used to make. Open for lunch and dinner. $–$$.

Chuy's. 1728 Barton Springs Road; (512) 474–4452. Chuy's takes great pride in being one of the strangest restaurants in town. With the name, you might expect Chinese food, but you'll get Tex-Mex in a funky decor featuring multitudes of those Elvis-on-black-velvet paintings. The food is great, but watch out for the spiciest dishes—they're ultra hot, even for seasoned Tex-Mex lovers. $.

Scholz Garten. 1607 San Jacinto; (512) 474–1958. Dine on burgers or chicken-fried steaks in the beer garden of this restaurant that dates from 1866. A popular hangout for legislative types. Open for lunch and dinner, Monday through Saturday. $–$$.

Katz's Deli and Bar. 618 West Sixth Street; (512) 472–2037. Since 1979, this deli has been an Austin tradition, upholding the boast, "We never klose." Around the clock you can enjoy bagels and lox, chicken soup with matzoh balls, homemade blintzes, or Reuben sandwiches. Open for breakfast, lunch, and dinner. $–$$.

Dan McKlusky's. 301 East Sixth Street; (512) 473–8924; www.danmckluskys.com. Steak lovers have long flocked to this downtown eatery for steaks, seafood, lamb, quail, and more. All served with a generous house salad and your preference of baked or fried potatoes, rice pilaf, or the fresh vegetable of the day. Open for dinner nightly. $$$.

Hut's Hamburgers. 807 West Sixth Street; (512) 472–0693. This lively diner serves up some of Austin's most popular burgers, just as it has since 1939. Choose from more than twenty types of burgers, or enjoy chicken-fried steak, salads, and a daily special. One of the specialties of the house is an order of Texas-size onion rings. Open for lunch and dinner daily. $.

County Line on the Hill. 6500 West Bee Cave Road; (512) 327–1742; www.county line.com. This popular barbecue eatery combines the menu fare of side-of-the-road joints with the elegance of a lakeside restaurant. Both indoor and outdoor tables are available; menu offerings include brisket, sausage, chicken, and more, accompanied by large side orders and homemade desserts. $$$.

Fonda San Miguel. 2330 West North Loop; (512) 459–4121; www.fondasanmiguel.com. Austin is home to many excellent Tex-Mex eateries, but this restaurant specializes in true Mexican cuisine, such as shrimp Veracruz and pescado al mojo de Ajo. $$$.

Green Pastures. 811 West Live Oak; (512) 444–4747. This South Austin eatery is a favorite for wedding receptions and power meals but also makes a romantic retreat. The restaurant is housed in a historic mansion and features continental fare. $$$.

Hudson's on the Bend. 3509 RR 620 North; (512) 266–1369; www.hudsonsonthebend .com. This well-known eatery is a favorite for those looking for continental fare with a Texas twist. Dishes such as smoked quail are prepared with a gourmet touch. The restaurant itself, located near Lake Travis's Mansfield Dam, is housed in a stone home surrounded by gardens. Reservations are suggested. $$$.

Jeffrey's. 1204 West Lynn; (512) 477–5584; www.jeffreysofaustin.com. One of the most noted Austin restaurants is Jeffrey's, known for its gourmet continental cuisine. $$$.

Matt's El Rancho. 2613 South Lamar Boulevard; (512) 462–9333. This restaurant is a longtime Austin favorite offering up traditional Tex-Mex as well as Mexican dishes. Both indoor and outdoor seating are available. $$–$$$.

Shoreline Grill. 98 San Jacinto Boulevard; (512) 477–3300; www.shorelinegrill.com. The place to be in Austin for downtown power lunches, the Shoreline Grill is also a romantic spot for sunset dinners. The restaurant overlooks Town Lake and is just blocks from the Convention Center. After a meal, diners can step out back and walk Town Lake's hike and bike trail or, during the warm weather months, see the evening exodus of the bats. $$$.

where to stay

Hyatt Regency Austin. 208 Barton Springs Road; (512) 477–1234; www.austin.hyatt .com. This 447-room hotel has a signature Hyatt lobby, with glass elevators, a flowing stream, and a beautiful view of Town Lake. $$$.

Four Seasons Hotel. 98 San Jacinto Boulevard; (800) 819–5053 or (512) 478–4500; www.fourseasons.com/austin. Located on the northern edge of Town Lake, this hotel offers a Southwestern atmosphere and a great view of the lake. Its back terrace is very popular with Austinites during the summer months, affording patrons one of the best looks at the city's famed Town Lake bat colony. $$$.

Driskill Hotel. 112 East Sixth Street; (800) 252–9367 or (512) 474–5911; www.driskill hotel.com. Built in 1886 by cattle baron Jesse Driskill, this is Austin's oldest hotel. Its 177 rooms and beautiful lobby recall an elegant age in the city's history. The hotel sits within easy walking distance of the State Capitol and the Sixth Street entertainment district. Two restaurants and bars offer food and refreshments to guests preferring to "stay in." $$$.

Lake Austin Spa Resort. 1705 South Quinlan Park Road; (800) 847–5637 or (512) 372–7300; www.lakeaustin.com. Perched on a quiet shore of Lake Austin in the rolling hills, the resort is casual elegance at its best. You'll find plenty of activity here in the form of aerobics classes on a suspended wood floor, tennis, dancing, mountain biking, and even sculling on the lake's calm waters. Activity goes hand-in-hand with relaxation, and here that means stress reduction sessions. For the ultimate in relaxation, enjoy a massage, facial, manicure, aloe vera body mask, invigorating sea salt scrub, or aromatherapy scalp conditioning. $$$.

Barton Creek Resort and Spa. 8212 Barton Club Drive; (800) 336–6158 or (512) 329–4000; www.bartoncreek.com. This luxurious resort is a favorite with golfers, offering fifty-four holes to challenge even the most dedicated player. Other amenities include a driving range, a putting green, lighted tennis courts, both indoor and outdoor pools, and more. $$$.

Holiday Inn Town Lake. 20 North I–35; (512) 472–8211; www.holiday-inn.com. Day-trippers who want to extend their excursion in Austin with a stay along Town Lake find this hotel relaxing and well located. Situated on the south banks of Town Lake just off I–35, the hotel includes a restaurant and bar as well as a pool. $$$.

Lakeway Resort and Spa. 101 Lakeway Drive (18 miles west of Austin on FM 620, off TX 71 on Lake Travis); (800) LAKEWAY; www.lakeway.dolce.com. This resort is a quiet getaway and a favorite with those looking for a weekend of boating, tennis, or golf. Rooms have private patios, many with great views of the lake. Amenities include thirty-six holes of golf, tennis, a tennis pro, boating, water sports, and more. $$$.

McCallum House. 613 West Thirty-second Street; (512) 451–6744. This historic bed-and-breakfast, once the home of Texas suffragette Jane McCallum, is in a convenient location for those looking to be near the University of Texas. The facility offers guests a full breakfast. Only older children are permitted to stay here, so check first. $$–$$$.

Marriott at the Capitol. 701 East Eleventh Street; (512) 478–1111; www.marriott.com. Want to be just a law book's throw from the State Capitol? Then this might just be the place for you. The hotel, which includes good city views, offers a restaurant, bar, pool, and more. $$$.

Renaissance Austin Hotel. 9721 Arboretum Boulevard; (512) 343–2626; www.marriott.com. Day-trippers who want to make their base on the northwest side of town find high-rise accommodations in this elegant hotel. Complete with an atrium lobby, the hotel is just steps away from the shops and restaurants of the Arboretum. $$$.

east

day trip 01

east

painted churches:
luling, flatonia,
praha, schulenburg

luling

You can leave San Antonio on either I–10 or US 90, traveling east past Seguin on your way to Luling. (For Seguin attractions, see East Day Trip 02.)

Luling is best known as an oil town. Oil was discovered here in 1922, and fields pumping this "black gold" can be seen throughout the Luling area. Even before that time the town had a reputation as "the toughest town in Texas," frequented by gunfighters such as John Wesley Hardin and Ben Thompson. Luling was also a cattle center and the end of a railroad line to Chihuahua, Mexico.

When oil was discovered, the economy of the town shifted to this profitable industry. Today 184 wells pump within the city limits. As part of a beautification effort, the chamber of commerce commissioned an artist to transform several of the pump jacks into moving sculptures in the shapes of cartoon characters. There's even a Santa Claus and a butterfly to brighten up the streets.

where to go

Palmetto State Park. Six miles southeast of town on US 183, then southwest on Park Road 11 for 2 miles, along the banks of the San Marcos River; (830) 672–3266; www.tpwd.state.tx.us. Palmetto State Park is a topographical anomaly amid gently rolling farm and ranch land. According to scientists, the river shifted course thousands of years

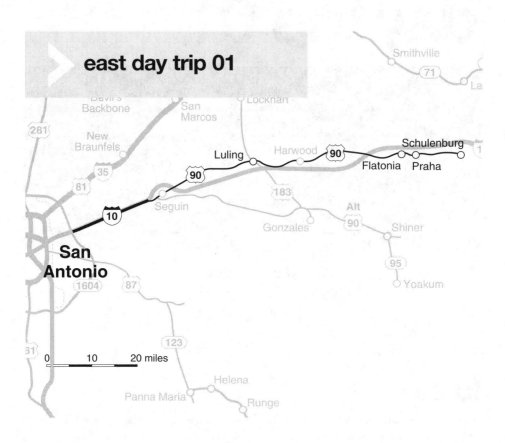

ago, leaving a huge deposit of silt. This sediment absorbed rain and groundwater, nurturing a marshy swamp estimated to be more than 18,000 years old. Now part of Palmetto State Park, the swamp is filled with palmettos as well as moss-draped trees, 4-foot-tall irises, and many bird species. Nature trails wind throughout the area.

The park has full hookups and tent sites. There's also picnicking. During the warmer months bring along mosquito repellent. Open daily. Fee.

Central Texas Oil Patch Museum & Luling Chamber of Commerce Visitors' Center. 421 Davis Street; (830) 875–3214. Luling's oil businesses, starting with Rafael Rios No. 1 (an oil field 12 miles long and 2 miles wide), are explored in this museum. Call for hours. Free.

where to eat

Luling City Market. 633 Davis Street; (877) LCM–BBQ1 or (830) 875–9019; www.luling citymarket.com. This is small-town barbecue the way it ought to be: served up in a no-frills meat market, with ambience replaced by local atmosphere. The Luling City Market turns out smoked brisket, sausage, and ribs. $.

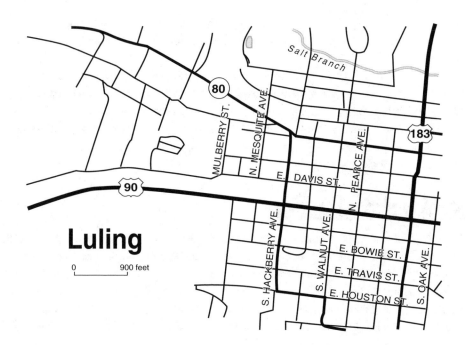

Luling

0   900 feet

flatonia

Return to US 90 and continue east to the small town of Flatonia. This community was settled by English, German, Bohemian, and Czech immigrants, many of whom came to the
United States in the 1850s and 1860s to avoid Austro-Hungarian oppression.

where to go

E. A. Arnim Archives and Museum. US 90, downtown; (512) 865–2451. This local-history
museum contains exhibits on Flatonia's early days and its settlement by many cultural
groups. Open Sunday afternoon. Free.

praha

Three miles east of Flatonia on US 90 is Praha (the Slovakian spelling for "Prague"). Like its
European counterpart, Praha holds a predominantly Czech population, descendants of
immigrants who came here in 1855.

  The main structure in Praha is the Assumption of the Blessed Virgin Mary Church, often
called St. Mary's. Built in 1895, it is one of a half dozen painted churches in the area.
Although few examples remain today, it was not unusual for nineteenth-century rural
churches to boast painted interiors. Guided tours from nearby Schulenburg visit all the

churches (to book a tour, call 866–504–5294), but you can see most of the structures on a self-guided trip. A free brochure and map is available from the Schulenburg Chamber of Commerce (409–743–4514).

St. Mary's has a beautifully painted vaulted ceiling, the work of Swiss-born artist Gottfried Flury. Never retouched, the 1895 murals on the tongue-and-groove ceiling depict golden angels high over a pastoral setting. This Praha church, as well as ones in High Hill and Ammannsville, are listed in the National Register of Historic Places. The churches are open Monday through Saturday 8:00 A.M. to 5:00 P.M., although it is not guaranteed that the doors will be unlocked at all times. Free.

schulenburg

Continue east on US 90 to the agricultural community of Schulenburg (meaning "school town" in German). Carnation Milk Company's first plant was built in Schulenburg in 1929, and even today dairy products generate a major source of income for the area. Schulenburg is known as the "Home of the Painted Churches," although the elaborately painted structures are actually located in nearby small communities (Dubina, Ammannsville, Swiss Alp, High Hill, and Praha). These beautifully painted buildings are reminders of the area's rural traditions and ethnic background.

In Ammannsville, the St. John the Baptist Church includes stained-glass windows illustrating the Czech heritage of the parish. High Hill's St. Mary's Church boasts marbleized

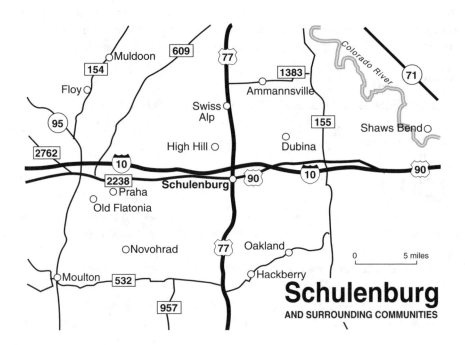

Schulenburg
AND SURROUNDING COMMUNITIES

columns, religious statuary, and a history of a European-style seating arrangement with women on the left and men on the right. The murals in Dubina's Sts. Cyril and Methodius Church were covered over during a 1952 remodeling. In 1981 the paintings, depicting winged angels and elaborate stencil patterns, were renovated by a local parishioner.

where to go

Painted Churches Tour. With a two- to three-week notice, the Schulenburg Chamber of Commerce (866–504–5294 or 409–743–4514) provides guides for groups of ten or more. You can always enjoy a self-guided tour; maps of the church locations are available from the chamber at 618 North Main Street. Fee for guided tour.

where to eat

Oakridge Smokehouse Restaurant. I–10 and TX 77; (800) 584–6325 or (979) 743–3372; www.oakridge-smokehouse.com. Hungry I–10 travelers between San Antonio and Houston know all about Oakridge Smokehouse. In business nearly half a century, this family-owned company churns out barbecue and sausage to please travelers and mail-order customers. The comfortable restaurant is popular with families, not just for its extensive menu but also for its large gift shop up front. $–$$.

day trip 02

east

suds and saddles:
seguin, gonzales,
shiner, yoakum

seguin

You can reach Seguin (pronounced "se-GEEN") via either US 90 or I–10 east of San Antonio. It's a 36-mile trip to this town on the Guadalupe River named for Lt. Col. Juan Seguin, a hero of the Texas Revolution. Prior to the Mexican invasion of 1837, Seguin was ordered by his superiors to destroy San Antonio. He refused, thus saving the city.

Many towns boast nicknames, from Austin's "River City" to San Antonio's "Alamo City." Seguin, though, has one of the most unusual: "The Mother of Concrete Cities." A Seguin chemist held several concrete production patents, accounting for the use of the material in more than ninety area buildings by the end of the nineteenth century.

The most beautiful area of Seguin is Starcke Park. It offers picnic tables under huge pecan, oak, and cypress trees and a winding drive along the Guadalupe River. The tree Seguin is best known for is the pecan. The town even calls itself the home of the "World's Largest Pecan," a statue located on the courthouse lawn at Court Street.

where to go

Chamber of Commerce. 427 North Austin Street; (800) 580–PECAN or (830) 379–6382. Stop by the chamber office for brochures and maps. Open weekdays.

Sebastopol State Historical Park. 704 Zorn Street; (830) 379–4833; www.tpwd.state
.tx.us. From I–35, take TX 123 South in San Marcos and follow Business 123 into Seguin.
Turn right onto Court Street to 704 Zorn. This is one of the best examples of the early use
of concrete in the Southwest.

Sebastopol was once a large home, constructed of concrete with a plaster overlay.
Today it is open for tours and contains exhibits illustrating the construction of this historic
building and its restoration in 1988. Tours are conducted weekends; call the chamber of
commerce to set up group tours at other times. Fee.

True Women Tours. Fans of Janice Woods Windle's *True Women* can take a guided tour of
the sites mentioned in this best-seller and seen in a television miniseries. Led by local
docents, the tours take a look at sites that play an important role in the historical novel: the
live-oak-shaded King Cemetery, the old First Methodist Church where two *True Women* characters were married, and the river bottom where horses were daringly rescued in the tale.

One of the most memorable stops is the Bettie Moss King Home, near the King
Cemetery. The home, with its wraparound porch and shady lawn, saw generations of the
King family and was also the childhood home of author Janice Woods Windle.

Call the Seguin Chamber of Commerce (800–580–PECAN) for tour times; a map for a
self-guided drive is also available at the chamber office (427 North Austin Street). Fee for
guided tour.

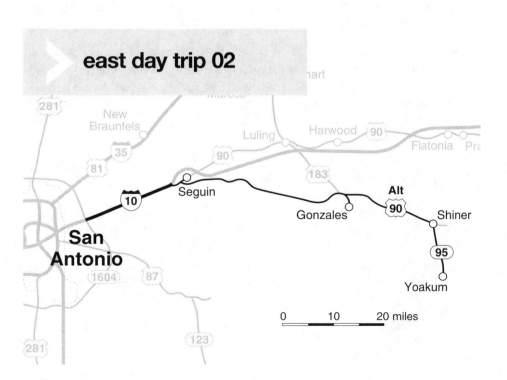

east day trip 02

Starcke Park. South side of town, off TX 123; (830) 401–2480. Make time for this pleasant park, where visitors can enjoy golf, tennis, and baseball as well as many riverside picnic spots. Large water park open seasonally. Free.

Seguin's Lakes. Seguin is surrounded by four lakes on the Guadalupe River that offer bass, crappie, and catfish fishing, including lighted docks for night fishing. RV facilities are available as well. The lakes include Lake Dunlap (I–10 to TX 46 exit west of Seguin, then 8 miles on TX 46), Lake McQueeney (I–10 to FM 78 exit, take FM 78 west for 3 miles to FM 725, then turn right and continue for 1 mile), Lake Placid (I–10 to FM 464 exit, stay on access road), and Meadow Lake (I–10 to TX 123 bypass, then south for 4 miles).

Los Nogales Museum. 415 South River, just south of the courthouse. The museum in Los Nogales, which means "walnuts" in Spanish, houses local artifacts. The small brick adobe building was constructed in 1849. Next door, the **Doll House** is filled with period children's toys you can see through the windows. This white miniature home was built between 1908 and 1910 by local cabinetmaker Louis Dietz as a playhouse for his niece. Later he used it to promote his business. For tour information call the chamber of commerce at (800) 580–7322.

Texas Theatre. 427 North Austin Street. This 1931 theater has been used for scenes in two movies: *Raggedy Man* and *The Great Waldo Pepper.* It still sports its original marquee and recalls the old days of small-town Texas theaters. For information call the chamber of commerce at (830) 379–6382.

Wave Pool. Starcke Park East; (830) 401–2482. In this Texas-size pool, youngsters can cool off under the Mushroom Shower or splash in the simulated waves. Nearby, the sprawling Kids Kingdom Playscape makes another excellent stop for energetic young travelers. Open seasonally.

biggest small-town celebration

Summer Seguin visitors should be ready for a red, white, and blue party known as the biggest small-town Fourth of July parade in Texas. The annual Freedom Fiesta has been drawing onlookers and participants since the early 1900s. Annual activities start in the morning with a patriotic parade, followed by food booths, arts and crafts, family entertainment, and kiddie rides for an old-fashioned street-fair atmosphere. In the evening, a street dance keeps the mood festive, as does a grand fireworks display in Max Starcke Park.

where to stay

Weinert House Bed and Breakfast. 1207 North Austin Street; (888) 303–0912 or (830) 303–0912; www.weinerthouse.com. Kick back and enjoy small-town life amid 1890s elegance in this historic Victorian home. Four guest quarters are decorated with period antiques. The Senator's Suite includes a fireplace and screened sunporch. $$. No credit cards.

gonzales

Take alternate US 90 (US 90A) east to Gonzales, one of Texas's most interesting historic cities. For many years this was the westernmost settlement in the state.

In 1831, the Mexican government gave a small brass cannon to Gonzales's citizens, as protection from constant Indian attacks. Four years later, when relations between Texas and Mexico soured, more than 150 Mexican soldiers staged a battle to retrieve the weapon. The soldiers were faced with eighteen Gonzaleans, who stalled the army while local citizens rolled out the small fieldpiece and prepared for action. Meanwhile, other townsfolk sewed the first battle flag of Texas, which pictured a cannon beneath the words "Come and Take It," a motto by which Gonzales is still known. The Texans fired the first shot, and the Mexican troops retreated. Although the confrontation was brief, this act began the Texas Revolution.

The site of this historic first conflict is marked by a monument located 7 miles southwest of Gonzales on TX 97. The first shots were fired a half mile north of the present monument.

where to go

Chamber of Commerce. 414 St. Lawrence Street; (830) 672–6532; www.gonzales texas.com. Located in the Old Jail Museum, this office has brochures on local attractions and events. Open weekdays.

Old Jail Museum. 414 St. Lawrence Street; (830) 672–6532 (chamber of commerce). This unusual museum is housed in the old Gonzales jail, built in 1887 and used until 1975. Downstairs you can tour the room where female prisoners and mentally ill persons once were incarcerated together. Exhibits include jail weapons created from spoons and bedsprings.

The walls of the second floor are chiseled with graffiti of past residents. The large room is rimmed with iron cells, all overlooking a reproduction of the old gallows that carried off its last hanging in 1921. According to legend, the prisoner continually watched the clocks on the adjacent courthouse, counting the hours he had left to live. He swore that he was innocent and said that if he were hanged the clocks would never keep accurate time again. Although the four clock faces have been changed since that time, none of them has ever kept the same time again. The museum is open daily (afternoons only on Sunday). Free.

Memorial Museum. 414 Smith Street, between St. Lawrence and St. Louis Streets; (830) 672–6350. This museum is dedicated to the history of Gonzales. Exhibits on the town's early days include the "Come and Take It" cannon. Open Tuesday through Sunday. Free.

Gonzales Pioneer Village. Half mile north of town on US 183; (830) 672–2157. This living-history center takes visitors back to Gonzales's frontier days. The village is comprised of log cabins, a cypress-constructed home, a grand Victorian home, a smokehouse, a blacksmith shop, and a church. The village also stages reenactments, including the Come and Take It celebration in October. Open weekends (and Fridays in summer months); group tours by appointment. Fee.

shiner

Continue east on US 90A for 18 miles to Shiner, best known as the home of Shiner beer, a Texas favorite produced by the tiny Spoetzl Brewery since 1909.

where to go

Spoetzl Brewery. 603 Brewery Street, off TX 95 North; (361) 594–3383; www.shiner.com. This tiny but historic brewery was founded in 1909 by Kosmos Spoetzl, a Bavarian brew-master. Here several Shiner beers are produced in one of the smallest commercial brew kettles in the country. Across the street, a museum and gift shop overflow with Shiner memorabilia, antiques, and photos of Spoetzl's early days. Free brewery tours on week-days at 11:00 A.M. and 1:30 P.M. Hospitality room open following tour. Free.

City Hall. US 90A, downtown; (512) 594–4180. This two-story building houses the fire department, police department, and city offices. Enter on the left side for city brochures and a free map.

Edwin Wolters Memorial Museum. 306 South Avenue I, off TX 95 South; (361) 594–3774. This museum is filled with home implements, weapons, fossils, and even a coun-try store representing the community's early days. Open weekdays as well as afternoons on the second and fourth Sunday of each month. Free.

where to stay

The Old Kasper House. 219 Avenue C; (361) 594–4336; www.oldkasperhouse.com. This bed-and-breakfast is located in the former home of cotton ginner John F. Kasper and his wife, Mary. Today the two-story Victorian home is a great small-town getaway, offering rooms with private baths. Nearby, other options include the Honeymoon Cottage, Czech Me Inn, Marenka's Cottage, and the Derrich Domov Inn, each with its own living and dining areas. All bedrooms have a private bath. $–$$.

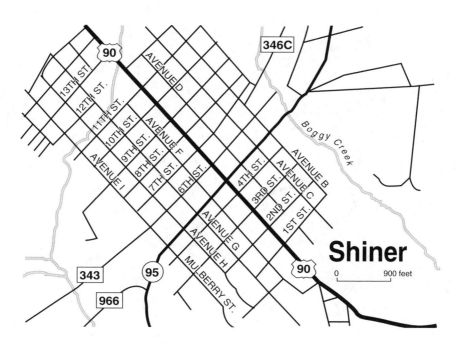

yoakum

From Shiner, drive south on TX 95 for 8 miles to US 77A. Turn right and continue for 2 miles. Yoakum was the starting point of many cattle drives along the Chisholm Trail, and in 1887 it became the junction for the San Antonio and Aransas Pass Railroad. When the railroad came to town, meat packinghouses followed. In 1919 the first tannery opened, producing leather knee pads for cotton pickers. Soon more leather businesses arrived, and eventually Yoakum earned its title as "the Leather Capital of the World."

Today twelve leather companies produce belts, saddles, bullwhips, gun slings, and wallets. Although the companies do not sell directly from their factories, the Leather Capital Store operates as a showroom and factory outlet for many Yoakum manufacturers. Tours of the leather companies are offered during the annual Land of Leather Days festival, the last weekend in February.

where to go

Yoakum Heritage Museum. 312 Simpson Street; (512) 293–7022. This two-story museum is filled with Yoakum memorabilia, from railroad paraphernalia to household items. The most interesting exhibit area is the Leather Room, with its displays on the leather factories. Open Tuesday, Thursday, Friday, and Sunday afternoons. Free.

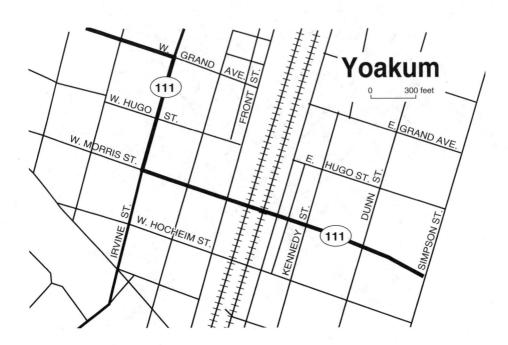

where to shop

The Leather Capital Store. 123 West Grand Street; (512) 293–9339. This shop is a leather museum and store rolled into one. Its display windows are painted with silhouettes of Texas history scenes. Inside, thousands of belts, purses, and boots—even gun slings and holsters—are offered for sale. Upstairs the facade of a Wild West village brightens a floor filled with saddles and Southwestern and western art. Deer shoulder blades etched with Indian scenes are produced by owner Leo Smith, who for many years worked as a commercial illustrator for one of the leather companies. Open Monday through Saturday.

Return home from Yoakum by retracing your steps or by heading north on TX 95 to Flatonia. From here, go west on either I–10 or US 90. Attractions on this stretch are covered in East Day Trip 01.

day trip 03

east

lost pines:
lockhart, bastrop, alum creek,
smithville, la grange

lockhart

To reach Lockhart, head east on I–10 to Seguin (see East Day Trip 02) and Luling (see East Day Trip 01), then turn north on US 183.

Lockhart is a conglomeration of the stuff of Texas legends: Indian battles, cattle drives, cotton, and oil. This small town, located 23 miles south of Austin on US 183, contains a state park and lots of history.

The biggest event in Lockhart's past was the Battle of Plum Creek in 1840. More than 600 Comanches raided the community of Linnville and were on their way home when they passed through this area. A group of settlers joined forces with the Tonkowa Indians to attack the Comanches, driving the Indians farther west and ending the Indian attacks in the region. This battle is reenacted every May at the Chisholm Trail Roundup.

Lockhart is also well known as the home of Mebane cotton. Developed by A. D. Mebane, this strain is resistant to the boll weevil, an insect that can demolish not only whole fields but entire economies as well.

where to go

Lockhart State Park. (512) 398–3479; www.tpwd.state.tx.us. Go 1 mile south of Lockhart on US 183 to FM 20, head southwest for 2 miles to Park Road 10, and continue 1 mile

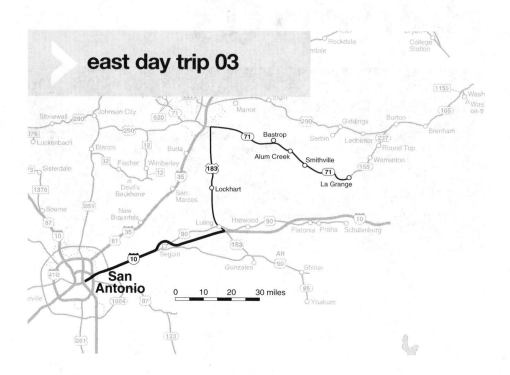

south. This 263-acre park has a nine-hole golf course, fishing on Plum Creek, picnic areas, a swimming pool, and campsites for both tents and trailers. Many of the facilities were built by the Civilian Conservation Corps in the 1930s. Open daily. Fee.

Dr. Eugene Clark Library. 217 South Main Street; (512) 398–3223. Built in 1889, this is the oldest continuously operating library in Texas. Modeled after the Villa Rotunda in Vicenza, Italy, it has stained-glass windows, ornate fixtures, and a stage where President William Taft once spoke. Open Monday through Saturday. Free.

where to eat

Kreuz Market. 619 North Colorado Street; (512) 398–2361; www.kreuzmarket.com. Vegetarians, head elsewhere. This barbecue restaurant is a meat-intensive kind of place, offering spicy sausage, pork loin, prime rib, and pork ribs, with a few side dishes such as German potatoes and sauerkraut. Open Monday through Saturday, early morning to evening; closed Sunday $–$$. No credit cards.

Black's Barbecue. 215 North Main Street; (512) 398–2712. This cafeteria-style restaurant is reputedly the oldest barbecue joint in Texas under the same ownership. Beef brisket is the specialty of the house, along with sausage, ribs, chicken, and ham. There's also a fully stocked salad bar. Open daily for lunch and dinner. $–$$. No credit cards.

bastrop

To reach Bastrop, drive north from Lockhart on US 183 to the intersection of TX 21. Turn east and continue to the intersection of US 71, then turn south and continue to Bastrop. Unlike the juniper-dotted hills to the west or the rolling farmland to the east, the Bastrop area is surrounded by a pine forest called Lost Pines. Here grows the westernmost stand of loblolly pines in America. Scientists believe that these trees were once part of the forests of East Texas, but climactic changes over the last 10,000 years account for the farmland now separating the Lost Pines from their cousins to the east.

Bastrop is one of the oldest settlements in the state, built in 1829 along the Camino Real, a road also known as the King's Highway or the Old San Antonio Road. This was the western edge of the "Little Colony" established by Stephen F. Austin. Settlers came by the wagonload from around the country to claim a share of this fertile land and to establish a home in this dangerous territory. Even as homes were being erected, Indian raids continued in this area for many years.

Bastrop is a popular day trip for Austinites looking for a chance to shop and savor some quiet country life in a historic setting. Outdoors lovers can enjoy two nearby state parks and also the Colorado River, which winds through the heart of downtown. Canoe rentals and guided trips along the river are available.

where to go

Chamber of Commerce. 927 Main Street; (512) 303–0558; www.bastropchamber.com. Stop by this office for maps and brochures, including "A Walking Tour of Historic Bastrop." The chamber of commerce also rents bicycles so you can pedal through these historic neighborhoods. If you'd rather see the town from the seat of a boat, give the chamber a call for details on guided canoe trips.

Lock's Drug. 1003 Main Street; (512) 321–2551. This turn-of-the-twentieth-century drugstore features an antique mirrored fountain where you can belly up for a thick, creamy malt. Built-in cabinets are still labeled with the names of their original contents, and old apothecary tools sit in the front windows. Open daily except Sunday.

Bastrop County Historical Society Museum. 702 Main Street; (512) 303–0057. This 1850 frame cabin contains Indian relics and pioneer exhibits. Open afternoons daily. Fee.

Bastrop State Park. TX 21, 1½ miles east of Bastrop; (512) 321–2101 for park information or (512) 389–8900 for reservations; www.tpwd.state.tx.us. Beautiful piney woods are the main draw at this 3,500-acre park, the fourth busiest state park in Texas. Facilities include a nine-hole golf course, campsites, and a ten-acre fishing lake. The 1930s-built stone and cedar cabins are very popular and should be booked well in advance. They feature fireplaces, bathrooms, and kitchen facilities. Guided bus tours every other Saturday during summer months introduce visitors to the park's unique ecology and to an endangered resident: the Houston toad. Fee.

Bastrop Opera House. 711 Spring Street; (512) 321–6283. Built in 1889, this building was once the entertainment center of town. After a major renovation in 1978, it's again the cultural center of Bastrop, the site for live theater ranging from mysteries to vaudeville. Call for show schedule.

Central Texas Museum of Automotive History. (512) 237–2635; www.ctmah.org. South on FM 304 to FM 535; left 1 mile to Rosanky. This private museum is dedicated to the collection and preservation of old cars and accessories. The vehicles on display include a 1935 Rolls Royce Phantom, a La France fire engine, and a 1922 Franklin. Open Friday through Sunday October to March; Wednesday through Sunday April to September. Fee.

McKinney Roughs Natural Science Lab. Twelve miles east of the Austin Bergstrom Airport on TX 71; (800) 776–5272; www.lcra.org. The entrance is located on the north side of TX 71. This day-use park offers restrooms, hike/bike trails, picnic facilities, and a canoe launch.

North Shore Park, Lake Bastrop. (800) 776–5272. Three miles east of Bastrop and 40 miles east of Austin. From Austin, take TX 71 east to Bastrop and travel north on TX 95. After 2 miles, turn right on FM 1441. Travel approximately 4 miles and the park entrance is on the right. Day travelers and overnight campers can still use the park. Facilities include campsites, RV sites, group pavilions, a two-lane boat ramp, a fishing pier, playgrounds, trails, and more. Open daily.

South Shore Park, Lake Bastrop. (800) 776–5272. Take TX 71 east to Bastrop and travel north on TX 95. After traveling about 1½ miles, take TX 21 east and travel about 3 miles to South Shore Road (CR 352). Turn left on South Shore Road. Park entrance is on right. This popular LCRA park includes restrooms, showers, a group facility, hike/bike trails, picnic facilities, and a boat ramp. Open daily.

where to shop

Park your car and enjoy an afternoon of browsing through the many antiques and specialty stores along Main Street.

Apothecary's Hall. 805 Main Street; (512) 321–3022. Shop for antiques ranging from collectibles to furniture in this downtown shop.

Old Town Emporium. 815 Main Street; (512) 321–3635. You'll find all kinds of crafts and specialty gifts in this large store.

alum creek

Continue east from Bastrop on TX 71, and soon you'll reach the crossing of Alum Creek. In 1828, this was the site of a fort used by several families during the area's most active Indian days. Years later this spot was used as a stagecoach stop. Today all that's left of the community of Alum Creek is a collection of more than a dozen antiques and junk shops. It's a fun stop for avid collectors. The shops are located on the left side of the road as you head east; many are open weekends only.

smithville

Continue east from Alum Creek on TX 71 to Smithville, a small town that's built alongside the railroad tracks at the edge of the piney woods and home of Buescher State Park. Smithville was once a ferry stop on the Colorado River. In the 1880s, the railroad replaced the ferries as the main mode of transportation, and tracks were laid across town. Today the railroad still plays an important part in Smithville's economy.

where to go

Jim Long Railroad Park Museum. 100 West First Street; (512) 237–2313. Built beside the tracks, this park has two cabooses and a depot relocated here from West Point, a community east of town. The chamber of commerce office is housed in the depot as well. Open weekdays; hours vary. Free.

Buescher State Park. (512) 237–2241; www.tpwd.state.tx.us. Three miles north of town via TX 71 and FM 2104, or access from Park Road 1. Buescher (pronounced "BISH-er") neighbors Bastrop State Park, but the two boast different environments. Oaks dominate this park, along with a few pines. The park is especially popular for its thirty-acre lake. Visitors can enjoy ample campsites and screened shelters, as well as a playground and picnic area. Fee.

Vernon L. Richards Riverbend Park. (800) 776–5272. TX 71 where it crosses the Colorado River, just north of Smithville. The park entrance is located off the highway shoulder on the westbound side of the highway. This LCRA park includes restrooms, a group facility, hike/bike trails, picnic facilities, and a boat ramp. Open daily.

Smithville Heritage Society Museum. 602 Main Street; (512) 237–4545. This 1908 home contains the Smithville archives and a museum of local memorabilia. Open Tuesday (call for other times). Free.

Rocky Hill Ranch Mountain Bike Resort. FM 153, 2 miles northeast of Buescher State Park; (512) 237–3112. Beginner, intermediate, advanced, and expert trails tempt mountain bikers with more than 1,200 acres that include gentle slopes and challenging grades as well as stream crossings. More than 30 miles of trails are available for use by helmeted riders. The ranch includes a casual restaurant with horseshoes, shuffleboard, and beach volleyball; campsites are available along small creeks and spring-fed water holes. Fee.

la grange

Just 4 miles southeast of Smithville on the left side of TX 71 is a scenic overlook, an excellent place to pull over for a picnic. While you're here you can gaze at the miles of rolling hills and farmland that attracted many German and Czech immigrants a century ago.

Continue on TX 71 to the infamous community of La Grange. For generations this was a quiet town in the center of a farming region. In the 1970s, however, La Grange caught the public's attention with the unveiling of the Chicken Ranch, a brothel that became the subject of the Broadway musical and movie *The Best Little Whorehouse in Texas*. Today the Chicken Ranch is gone, but La Grange still has other sights to see.

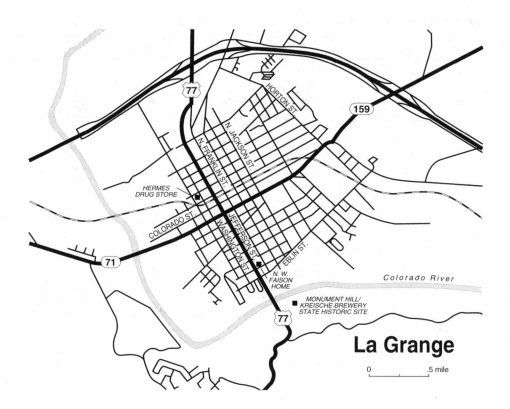

La Grange

> ## the chicken ranch

La Grange drew international attention in 1973 when the story of what many believe was the country's oldest continuously run brothel was exposed by consumer-affairs reporter Marvin Zindler from KTRK-TV in Houston. The report would inspire a Broadway musical and movie as well as lot of curiosity about the site, which was located on eleven acres outside of La Grange. The house, which was added onto many times as the number of women increased, was nicknamed the Chicken Ranch during the Great Depression. When customers grew fewer, the proprietor, a woman known as Miss Jessie, began allowing men to pay in chickens. Soon the ranch was overrun with poultry and eggs, both of which they sold locally.

As economic times improved, the ranch returned to a cash basis, and ownership changed in 1952 to a madam who became one of La Grange's largest philanthropists.

When the Chicken Ranch closed, the building was moved to Dallas and, for a while, became a chicken restaurant.

where to go

Monument Hill/Kreische Brewery State Historic Site. US 77, 1 mile south of La Grange; (409) 968–5658; www.tpwd.state.tx.us. Located on a bluff high above town, this site is the home to two combined parks.

Monument Hill Historical Park is the burial site for the Texans who died in the Dawson Massacre and the Mier Expedition, two historic Mexican conflicts that occurred in 1842, six years after the Texas Revolution. The Dawson Massacre took place near San Antonio when La Grange citizen Nicholas Dawson gathered Texans to halt the continual Mexican attacks. Dawson's men were met by hundreds of Mexican troops, and thirty-five Texans were killed.

The Mexican village of Mier was attacked in a retaliatory move, resulting in the capture of Texas soldiers and citizens by Mexican general Santa Anna, who ordered every tenth man to be killed. The Texans were blindfolded and forced to draw beans: 159 of them white and 17 black. Men who drew white beans were imprisoned; those who drew black ones were executed.

The Kreische Brewery State Historical Site recalls a far more cheerful time in Texas history. Heinreich Kreische was a German who immigrated here from Europe. In 1849 he purchased the hilltop and the adjoining land, including the burial ground of those Texas heroes, for his brewery site. Before closing the brewery in 1884, Kreische became the third largest beer producer in the state. Open daily until 5:00 P.M. Fee (one admission covers both adjacent sites).

Oak Thicket Park. (979) 249–3504; www.lcra.org. Take TX 71 to La Grange; from La Grange travel east on TX 159 for about 7 miles. Turn right at the sign for Fayette County Lake. This sixty-five-acre park offers plenty of family-oriented activities: a playground, fishing piers, and a good swimming area on Lake Fayette. Camping is available, as well as eight cabins.

Park Prairie Park. (979) 249–3504; www.lcra.org. Take TX 71 to La Grange; from La Grange travel 10 miles east on TX 159 to the entrance of the park. Park Prairie is another favorite with families, thanks to volleyball courts, plenty of picnic space, tent camping, and even some pelicans and gulls along the shores of Lake Fayette. Hikers can walk to Oak Thicket Park on a 3-mile trail. Other facilities include restrooms, showers, a group facility, and a boat ramp.

White Rock Park. On east bank of Colorado River, just south of La Grange. From La Grange take US 77 (Jefferson Street) south to Elbin Road and continue about ¾ mile to Mode Lane (CR 134). Take a right on Mode Lane and travel about ¼ mile. Park entrance is on right. This day-use park includes restrooms, hike/bike trails, picnic facilities, and a canoe launch.

Hermes Drug Store. 148 North Washington Street; (409) 968–5835. Established in 1856, this is the oldest drugstore in continuous operation in Texas. Visitors can see authentic old-time structures, beveled mirrors, and more. Open Monday through Saturday.

N. W. Faison Home. 822 South Jefferson Street; (800) 524–7264. N. W. Faison was a survivor of both the Dawson Massacre and the Mier Expedition in 1842. The Faison family resided in this home for more than twenty years, and today it contains the family's furniture as well as exhibits from the Mexican War. Open by appointment. Fee.

southeast

day trip 01

southeast

texas history:
panna maria, helena,
runge, goliad

panna maria

To reach Panna Maria, leave San Antonio southeast on US 87. At the intersection of TX 123, drive south past the tiny Polish communities of Kosciusko and Cestohowa. At the intersection of FM 81, turn left for the 1-mile drive to Panna Maria.

If you weren't aware of its interesting history, you might just call this another pint-size Texas town, perched on a shady hilltop with a nice breeze and a beautiful view. But there's a lot more to Panna Maria, which means "Virgin Mary" in Polish, than meets the eye. This quiet community was the first Polish settlement in America, and it still maintains a place in the history of Poland, well known among the people of the old country.

This small town was founded in 1854 by one hundred Polish families led by Father Leopold Moczygemba. After a nine-week voyage to Galveston, the settlers rented Mexican carts to transport their farm tools and bedding as well as the cross from their parish church. They made the difficult journey to central Texas on foot, finally stopping at the hillside that overlooks the San Antonio River and Cibolo Creek. The day was December 24, 1854, and the pioneers offered a midnight mass beneath one of the large hilltop oaks. They settled here.

The year that followed was a grueling one, a time when the pioneers learned the harshness of their new home. A cold winter was followed by a hot, dry summer filled with snakes and insects. Most of the settlers did succeed with their new venture and were soon joined by more Polish immigrants.

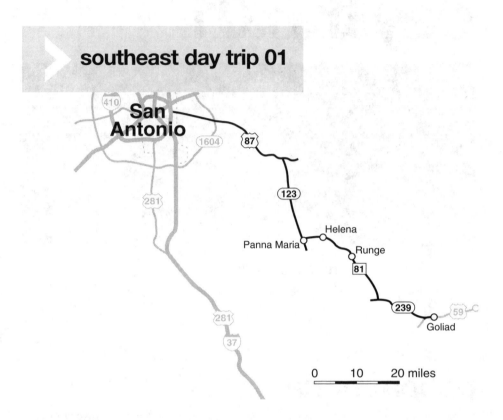

where to go

Church of the Immaculate Conception. TX 81, in town; no phone. Within two years of settling in Panna Maria, the pioneers built the Church of the Immaculate Conception, the first Polish church in America. The original church was destroyed by fire and replaced in 1878 by the present structure, which serves as the center of worship for Panna Maria's citizens.

The church is home to a replica of the mosaic of Our Lady of Czestochowa, or the Black Madonna. The original Black Madonna is enshrined at the Monastery of Jasna Gora in Czestochowa, Poland, a city about 65 miles east of the area from which the first Panna Maria pioneers originated. According to tradition, the Madonna was painted by St. Luke and then found in the Holy Land in A.D. 326 by Saint Helena, mother of Constantine the Great.

This replica, a gift to the United States from Poland, was presented to the town by President Johnson in 1966. It rests on display at the front of the church along with hand-carved chairs and a gold chalice that belonged to Pope John Paul II. These priceless treasures were presented to the people of Panna Maria in 1987.

The church is open daily. For a small donation you can purchase a brochure outlining the history of the Black Madonna and Panna Maria's early settlers. Free.

helena

From Panna Maria, continue on FM 81 for 5 miles to the tiny community of Helena. This was once a thriving town on the San Antonio River, founded in 1852 by Thomas Ruckman and Louis Owings (the latter became the first governor of the Arizona territory). Owings named the town after his wife, Helen.

During the Civil War, much of the Confederate cotton passed through the town. At the time, Helena even had its own Confederate post office, which issued Helena stamps. Today they're a rare find, worth several thousand dollars each. Helena's existence as a thriving burg came to a halt in 1886 when the railroad bypassed the town. Soon the county seat moved to Karnes City, and the town all but rolled up the sidewalks.

where to go

Karnes County Museum. FM 81; (830) 780–3210. This museum is actually a collection of historic buildings from the area, including a post office, jail, farmhouse, and barn. A museum traces the history of Karnes County, including its busy days during the Civil War. The grounds, shaded by large mesquite trees, also provide a picnic area. Open Tuesday through Saturday. Free.

runge

From Helena, continue on TX 81 for 9 miles to Runge, population 1,139. This community was founded by settlers from Panna Maria, who located it on the Texas and New Orleans Railroad line. Today it's a quiet farming community.

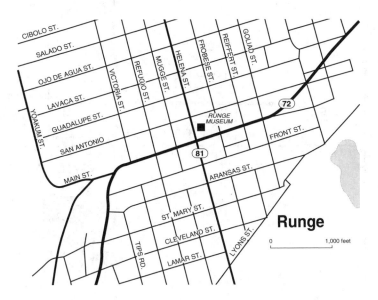

where to go

Runge Museum. 106 North Helena; (830) 239–4289. A few years ago this museum burned, but the collection, like the town of Runge itself, has persevered. Community residents pitched in their time and put a new roof on a historic structure that had served as a general store. Today this small museum contains exhibits on life in Runge during the 1880s. Set up like an old general store, it's filled with historic photos and items from Runge's past, including old-fashioned irons and household goods. Call for hours. Free.

goliad

To reach Goliad, continue southeast from Panna Maria on FM 81 past the communities of Helena and Runge, both of which were once thriving towns. Take TX 239 south at Charco to the intersection of US 59, then head east to the historic city of Goliad.

Like the Alamo and the Battle of San Jacinto, Goliad holds a special place in Texas history. Founded by the Spanish, Goliad is the third oldest city in Texas. To protect their passage to the Gulf, the Spaniards moved their Mission Espíritu Santo and its royal protector, Presidio La Bahia (Fort of the Bay), to this location in 1749. At that time the community was named Santa Dorotea. Years later, the town's name was changed to Goliad, an anagram of the spoken word Hidalgo (the *h* is silent in Spanish). Hidalgo was a priest who became a hero during the Mexican Revolution.

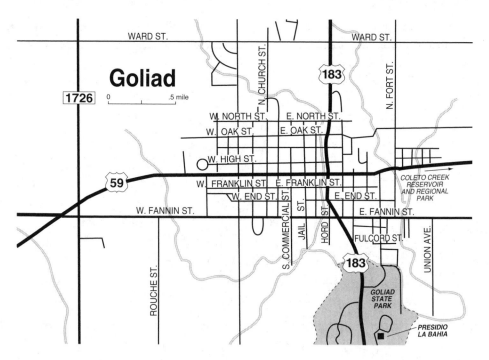

Few towns have their own flag, but Goliad boasts its own historic, if somewhat grue-some, banner. On October 9, 1835, the Texas colonists made a move in their battle for inde-pendence. The settlers took over the presidio and raised the "Bloody Arm Flag," picturing a severed arm holding a sword.

The next year the Texans, led by Col. James W. Fannin Jr., surrendered at the Battle of Coleto about 9 miles east of town. Approximately 390 soldiers were marched back to the presidio. After a week of imprisonment, all but twenty soldiers (physicians and mechanics) were placed before a firing squad. More than two dozen men escaped during the massacre, but 342 were killed, the largest loss of life during the fight for independence. "Remember Goliad" soon became a cry alongside "Remember the Alamo."

Today the presidio and the Mission Espíritu Santo are restored and open to the public. You also can visit Colonel Fannin's grave and see the monument that marks the resting place of the Texas soldiers.

where to go

Goliad State Historical Park. On US 183, ¼ mile south of town; (361) 645–3405; www .tpwd.state.tx.us. The highlight of this 178-acre park is the Mission Espíritu Santo. The restored mission offers spinning, weaving, and pottery-making demonstrations, primarily on weekends. Park activities feature hiking, picnicking, fishing, and boating. Screened shelters as well as tent and RV camping sites are available year-round. Fee.

Presidio La Bahia. US 183, south of the San Antonio River; (361) 645–3752; www.presidio labahia.org. The presidio holds many titles: It is the oldest fort in the West, one of few sites west of the Mississippi that was active in the American Revolution, the only fully restored Spanish presidio, and the only Texas Revolution site with its original appearance intact. The stone garrison is impressive and worth a stop. While you're here, visit the fort chapel, built in the Spanish colonial style. Open daily. Fee.

General Zaragoza Birthplace. Across from Presidio La Bahia; (361) 645–3405. This mod-est structure was the first home of Mexican general Ignacio Zaragoza. Under Zaragoza's command, the Mexican army defeated the French at the Battle of Puebla, an event now cel-ebrated as Cinco de Mayo or "Fifth of May" throughout Texas and Mexico. Today the build-ing is filled with exhibits that depict the general's role in Mexican history. Open Friday through Sunday; call for hours. Free.

Grave of Colonel Fannin and Troops. Just east of Presidio La Bahia; no phone. A large memorial marks the site of the massacre that occurred here on March 27, 1836. Free.

Market House Museum. 205 South Market; (361) 645–8767. This museum contains exhibits on local history. The building also houses the Goliad Chamber of Commerce, where you can pick up brochures and area maps. Open Wednesday through Saturday. Free.

Coleto Creek Reservoir and Regional Park. 15 miles northeast of Goliad on US 59; (361) 575–6366; www.coletocreekpark.com. This 3,100-acre reservoir is a South Texas mecca for boaters, fishers, and campers. Winter Texans can enjoy an extended stay at these campgrounds. Fee.

where to eat

La Bahia Restaurant. US 183, south of Presidio La Bahia; (361) 645–3651. Like its name suggests, this restaurant serves Mexican food, from fajitas to tacos, as well as a good selection of steaks and seafood. $–$$.

Empresario Restaurant. On the courthouse square; (361) 645–2347. Grab a deli sandwich followed by a slice of homemade pie at this eatery that's a favorite with locals. Open for lunch daily and Thursday through Saturday for dinner. $–$$.

day trip 02

southeast

gulf shores:
fannin, victoria, port lavaca,
indianola, port o'connor

fannin

Follow Southeast Day Trip 01 through Goliad, and then turn north on US 59 in Goliad. Follow US 59 to Fannin, a town of only ninety-four residents.

Named for James W. Fannin Jr., a hero of the Texas Revolution, the town is home to the Fannin Battleground State Historic Site, a site of interest to those tracing the history of the revolution in towns such as Goliad and Gonzales.

where to go

Fannin Battleground State Historic Site. One mile south of town on Park Road 27; (361) 645–2020; www.tpwd.state.tx.us. At this site, Col. James W. Fannin Jr. surrendered to the Mexican army after the Battle of Coleto Creek. The Mexican commander offered a clemency petition; General Santa Anna overruled the offer and ordered Fannin and his 342 men to be executed in Goliad. Today the men are remembered with a monument that recalls the actions of March 27, 1836. Picnic and restroom facilities are available at the day-use park. Open daily. Fee.

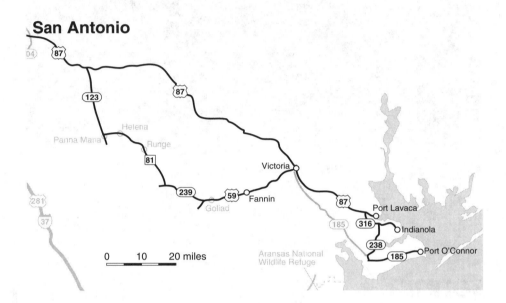

> ## southeast day trip 02

victoria

Termed "the Crossroads of Texas," Victoria is located equal distances from San Antonio, Austin, Houston, and Corpus Christi. Named for the first president of Mexico, the city was founded by forty-one Spanish families. Later the town became one of the first three towns incorporated by the Republic of Texas.

where to go

Coleto Creek Reservoir and Park. Fifteen miles west of Victoria off TX 59 South; (361) 575–6366; www.coletocreekpark.com. Swim, picnic, or camp at this year-round park. Sites with electricity are available; the park includes restrooms with showers, laundry facilities, barbecue pits, volleyball courts, and more. Fee.

McNamara Historical Museum. 502 North Liberty Street; (361) 575–8227. Learn more about the history of this region at this 1876 Victorian home. Open Tuesday through Sunday afternoons. Fee.

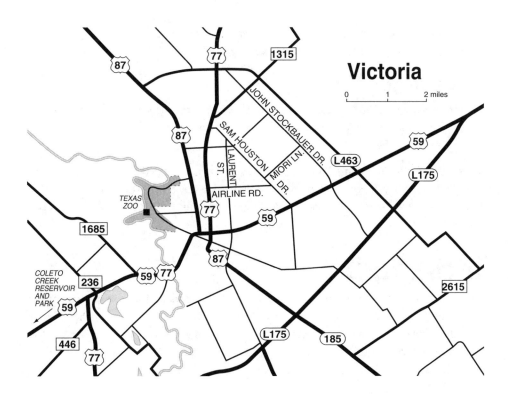

The Texas Zoo. 110 Memorial Drive; (361) 573–7681; www.texaszoo.org. More than 200 native Texas species of mammals, birds, reptiles, fish, and amphibians are included at this unique zoo. Endangered Texas species are highlighted. Texas species are also showcased in a native plants and wildflower garden. In 1984, the mission of the zoo was recognized by the state legislature, and it proclaimed this "the National Zoo of Texas." Open daily. Fee.

where to eat

The Lost Cajun. 700 Coleto Park Road; (361) 573–5751. Roll up your sleeves and get ready for some spicy Cajun food and all the fixin's at this restaurant. Open for dinner only Tuesday through Friday; lunch and dinner weekends. $–$$.

port lavaca

Continue south on US 87 for 25 miles to the bayside city of Port Lavaca. This community of about 12,000 residents, located on Lavaca Bay, is a center for fishing and agriculture but also contains some visitor attractions. The region is a favorite with bird lovers and beach buffs, who will find miles of beaches at several parks. Birders also enjoy the challenge of this destination, which is home to eight birding sites along the Great Texas Coastal Birding Trail. Anglers also find plenty of activity with several bay charters.

where to go

Formosa Wetlands Walkway and Lighthouse Beach. This beach park is a favorite with beach buffs as well as birders, who can view species from the walkway and the Alcoa Bird Tower. Open daily. Free.

Port Lavaca State Fishing Pier. 202 North Virginia; (361) 552–5311. This state facility, operated by the city of Port Lavaca, extends into Lavaca Bay and offers anglers the chance to enjoy saltwater fishing. The park includes a lighted pier as well as a restroom, snack bar, and fish-cleaning facility. Open daily.

indianola

Drive south on TX 316 for 14 miles to the ghost town of Indianola. This port city was one of the most prosperous in Texas during its heyday, before it began battling a series of tragedies. The city endured several yellow fever epidemics as well as shelling during the Civil War, only to finally be wiped out during a terrible hurricane in 1875 followed by another just more than a decade later. Today little remains of the ghost town.

where to go

Indianola County Historic Park. TX 316. This bayside park is located at the site of the former town and offers picnic sites, camping, fishing, and a boat ramp. Open daily. Fee.

port o'connor

This coastal community of just more than 1,000 residents is just about the end of the road; from here Texas gives way to the Gulf of Mexico. Port O'Connor is a destination for many anglers as well as birders. The commercial fishing center is also the gateway to Matagorda Island State Park. To reach Port O'Connor from Indianola, return north on TX 316 to the intersection of TX 238. Turn south on TX 238 to FM 1289, turn south again, and continue 11 miles to TX 185. Turn east and continue to Port O'Connor.

where to go

Matagorda Island State Park. Sixteenth Street and Intercoastal Canal; (361) 983–2215. Unlike most parks, this site can be reached only by ferry (Thursday through Sunday only) or another boat from Port O'Connor. This barrier island offers visitors primitive beach camping and use of several boat ramps. The park itself is little improved, with no electricity or drinking water. Its attractions include the chance to view more than 300 species of birds, including the whooping crane, that migrate through the region. Fishing and a quiet day at the beach are also popular activities. Open daily. Fee.

south

day trip 01

south

feathers and fins:
aransas pass, port aransas,
rockport-fulton

Birders come from around the world to test their skill at spotting some of the nearly 500 species recorded in this area. Anglers and spring-breakers also call this region a favorite.

aransas pass

To reach Aransas Pass, take I–37 south from San Antonio for 145 miles to Corpus Christi. (For attractions in Corpus Christi, see South Day Trip 02.) Cross the Harbor Bridge and follow US 181 north to TX 35. Continue to the intersection of TX 361, then turn right to Aransas Pass.

Aransas Pass is more a genuine fishing village and less a tourist destination than many other coastal communities. Most of its 8,000 residents are employed in the fishing industry. Make your first stop the chamber of commerce at 452 Cleveland Boulevard. This office can direct you to the Conn Brown Harbor for a look at the enormous shrimp fleet. The Seamen's Memorial Tower, a monument to the fishermen lost at sea, marks the entrance to the working harbor.

Nicknamed Saltwater Heaven, Aransas Pass is a popular stop with anglers eager to try their luck landing a speckled trout, redfish, flounder, black drum, or sheepshead in the bay. Deep-sea excursions are available as well as guides for fishing the saltwater flats and the bay.

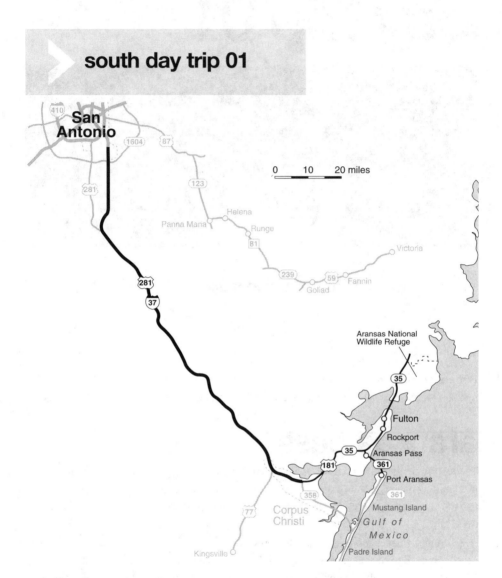

port aransas

To reach Port Aransas, follow TX 361 from Aransas Pass across the Redfish Bay Causeway to Harbor Island. Look north to see a restored, privately owned lighthouse, one of the few functioning lighthouses on the coast.

Port Aransas, or just Port A to most Texans, is perched on the northern tip of Mustang Island. Life in the coastal community centers around the Gulf, with its crying gulls, rolling surf, and miles of pancake-colored sand. When the spring-break crowds depart, it's a town that appeals to birders and anglers as much as to bikini-clad sunbathers.

Although Port A is now one of the state's most popular coastal destinations, its history as a hideaway dates from far before the days of sunscreen and surfboards. Some of the island's first residents were the fierce Karankawa Indians, a cannibalistic tribe that greeted later visitors, from pirates to Spanish missionaries. Buccaneer Jean Lafitte reputedly camped on the shores of Mustang Island, building bonfires to lure ships onto the beach to be looted and plundered. Wild horses, evolved from the steeds of Spanish explorers, gave Mustang Island its name.

Just as it was more than 200 years ago, the most common way to reach Port A is by water. As noted previously, you follow TX 361 from Aransas Pass across the Redfish Bay Causeway to Harbor Island. Five free ferries run twenty-four hours daily from Harbor Island across the Corpus Christi Ship Channel to Port Aransas. Tune your radio to 530 AM for ferry traffic conditions during the morning, lunch hour, and late afternoon rush times.

Port Aransas is a small town filled with year-round seaside attractions. During spring break, Port A greets more than 150,000 college students (and an increasing number of families as well) from throughout the Midwest and Southwest. The crowds are very manageable the rest of the year, however. During the winter months, most visitors are anglers and Winter Texans.

Port A tempts travelers with excellent attractions, dining, and shopping, and the best way to enjoy them is aboard the Port A Shuttle. This free trolley whisks vacationers from the community's many seaside restaurants and eclectic shops to the beach and Fisherman's Wharf.

From here you can spend an afternoon out in the Gulf aboard a deep-sea fishing cruise. These large group excursions take as many as one hundred passengers and provide bait and tackle. Serious anglers looking for big game fish such as marlin and shark should book charter excursions for personalized service.

A fishing cruise is great for a look at the Gulf. Trips include bait and tackle and cost about $50–$70 a day. Contact the tourist and convention bureau at (800) 45–COAST or (361) 749–5919 for more information.

After a day of surf hopping and sand-castle building, head to the town of Port Aransas itself. Shopping for shirts, shells, or elegant jewelry is a prime activity. So is dining. You can buy shrimp and fresh fish and prepare it in a condo kitchen or visit one of the island's many restaurants.

where to go

University of Texas Marine Science Institute. On Ship Channel; (361) 749–6711. Students of oceanography, ecology, marine chemistry, and botany train at this branch of the University of Texas, located on eighty-two beachfront acres. The visitor center is open to the public, featuring exhibits and films on Texas Gulf life. Open weekdays. Free.

Gulf Beach. The best way to learn about the beach life is to become part of it. And that's just what most visitors do. Armed with sunscreen, beach umbrellas, and folding chairs, they line the Gulf beach. Swimmers and surfers frequent the shallow, warm waters, and beachcombers search for fragile sand dollars, pieces of coral, and unbroken shells. Drivers on the public beach are restricted to a marked lane, and parking requires an annual permit, available for $6.00 from the chamber of commerce or at many Port Aransas businesses. There is free boardwalk access to the beach from many of the condominiums as well.

Mustang Island State Park. Park Road 53, southwest of Port Aransas; (361) 749–5246. The facilities at this scenic beach include freshwater showers, picnic tables, and tent and RV camping. The area is protected from vehicular traffic. Open daily. Fee.

San Jose Island. Woody's Boat Basin; (361) 749–5252. Both Port Aransas and Mustang Island State Park beaches are popular with vacationers, but if you're looking for a real getaway, head to nearby San Jose Island. You'll feel like pirate Jean Lafitte, whose camp was found on the island in 1834. Large iron rings, thought to have been used to tie up small boats his group used to row ashore, were discovered at the site. Even today, the island is accessible only by boat, and there are no public facilities.

San Jose is a quiet getaway for fishing, beachcombing, swimming, or shelling. Ferries leave throughout the day from Woody's Boat Basin, so you can stay as long as you like. Open daily. Fee.

Fishing Cruises. Few coastal cities offer more fishing cruises than Port Aransas. In varying seasons, the Gulf is home to mackerel, ling, pompano, marlin, barracuda, grouper, and amberjack. In the calmer bay waters, look for redfish, speckled trout, drum, and flounder.

Large group trips, taking as many as one hundred passengers, provide bait and tackle and cost about $50–$70 a day. A fishing license is not required for the deep-sea excursions since you will be fishing in out-of-state waters. These big cruises are great for families and budget travelers; serious anglers looking for big game fish such as marlin and shark should book charter excursions for personalized service.

If you do take a fishing cruise, be aware that Gulf waters can be very choppy. Except for the bay cruises, most boats travel 15 to 20 miles from shore. Seas are usually calmest in the summer, but even then 4- to 6-foot waves are possible. Seasickness has spoiled more than one vacationer's cruise, so be sure to purchase motion sickness medication or obtain a skin patch from your doctor before your trip.

For information on Port Aransas's many charters, contact the tourist and convention bureau at (800) 45–COAST or (361) 749–5919.

M/V Wharf Cat. Fisherman's Wharf; (800) 605–5448 or (361) 749–5448. This 75-foot heated and air-conditioned catamaran departs from Fisherman's Wharf every day from November through March for a look at magnificent whooping cranes. (On other days, the cruise departs from nearby Rockport.) The cruise leaves Port Aransas for the Aransas

National Wildlife Refuge, the winter home of the 5-foot-tall whooping cranes. Binoculars and scopes are provided (although it is best to bring your own), along with checklists of frequently spotted birds. Fee.

***Island Queen* Cruises.** Woody's Boat Basin; (361) 749–5252. This converted ferryboat offers bay fishing for speckled trout and redfish. Your ticket includes rod, reel, and tackle. You'll need a Texas fishing license. Call for seasonal schedule. Fee.

M/V *Texas Treasure*. (866) GOT–LUCK; www.txtreasure.com. The M/V *Texas Treasure* sails daily from Port Aransas and offers onboard gaming. While making the 9.2-mile cruise out to international waters, you can visit one of the five lounges, enjoy complimentary bingo, listen to some Caribbean tunes from the live band, or keep an eye out for dolphins from the lido deck. Once the ship reaches international waters, the action begins with slots and numerous table games. Identification is required to board, and all guests must be age twenty-one or older.

***The Duke* Cruise.** Woody's Boat Basin; (361) 749–5252. This boat cruises the channel, and often dolphins frolic alongside. A net collects marine life for visitors to view.

Travelers can take a two-hour nature tour to watch dolphins and birds. A trawl net pulls up shrimp, fish, crabs, squid, and other small marine creatures for a close-up look at the Gulf's wildlife. Birding tours to Shamrock Island, a protected rookery island, and Pelican Island, the largest brown pelican rookery island in Texas, are other favorite choices. Families enjoy the dolphin watch, a one-hour tour scheduled throughout the day. Other cruises departing from Woody's Sport Center include a sunset cruise and a sightseeing tour with a look at the U.S. Naval Station (home of the largest U.S. minesweeping fleet), the Lydia Ann Lighthouse, and the Intracoastal Waterway. Fee.

Port Aransas Birding Center. Off Cut-Off Road on Ross Avenue; (800) 45–COAST. This city is home to the Port Aransas Birding Center, part of the Great Texas Coastal Birding Trail. The center is landscaped with plants to attract migrating hummingbirds and is also home to a 6-foot alligator and a family of nutria, members of the rodent family who nest in fallen reeds. Free.

where to eat

The Crazy Cajun. 315 Alister Street; (361) 749–5069. This Cajun seafood restaurant's house specialty is a steaming concoction of shrimp, sausage, potatoes, stone crab claws, and crawfish in season. The bowl is dumped onto your butcher-paper tablecloth. The atmosphere is casual and fun, and there's live entertainment many nights. Open for lunch and dinner on weekends, dinner only on weekdays; closed Monday after Labor Day. $$.

Seafood and Spaghetti Works. 710 Alister Street; (361) 749–5666. This excellent restaurant is housed in a geodesic dome. Spaghetti primavera, shrimp and pepper pasta (a spicy dish that could be called Italian Tex-Mex if there were such a thing), filet mignon, and Cajun-style blackened redfish are popular choices. Save room for the Butterfinger cheesecake. Open for dinner only. $$.

Trout Street Bar and Grill. 104 West Cotter; (361) 749–7800. Enjoy the catch of the day and other seafood favorites at this restaurant. Burgers and steaks served along with oysters, shrimp, and the local catch. $$.

where to stay

You won't find full-service hotels in Port Aransas, but the town does offer everything from luxury condominium complexes to mom-and-pop motels aimed at vacationing anglers. Many condominiums include full kitchens and appliances and boardwalk access to the beach.

Sand Castle Condominiums. Sand Castle Drive; (800) 727–6201. This six-story condominium complex is located near the beach. Every room offers a great view and comes with a fully equipped kitchen. (If you can afford it, get a room with a private balcony.) When you've had enough saltwater swimming, take a dip in the large free-form pool in the center of the complex. Minimum stay and deposit required. $$$.

Tarpon Inn. 200 East Cotter Street; (800) 365–6784 or (361) 749–5555; www.thetarpon inn.com. The most historic hotel on the island (and listed on the National Register of Historic Places) is the Tarpon Inn, which dates from 1923. The lobby walls are papered with thousands of tarpon scales, each autographed by the lucky angler. There's even one signed by Franklin Roosevelt. Within the last few years, the hotel has been renovated, but it still has a breezy atmosphere with rockers on the verandas. Each of the twenty-four rooms is decorated and furnished with antiques. $$.

Dunes Condominiums. 1000 Lantana; (877) 296–3863 or (361) 749–5155; www.the dunescondos.com. These Gulf-view condominiums include kitchenettes with refrigerators and amenities such as a pool, a beach, and tennis. $$–$$$.

especially for winter texans

Port Aransas offers many activities for Winter Texans, from aerobic classes to potluck dinners. Condominiums offer special monthly off-season rates. For a calendar of events or information on rentals, call (800) 452–6278.

rockport-fulton

To reach the Rockport-Fulton area, return to Aransas Pass and take TX 35 north for 11 miles. The adjoining fishing villages of Rockport and Fulton lie along scenic Aransas Bay and are havens for snowbirds of all varieties, from 5-foot-tall whooping cranes to those in 30-foot-long Winnebagos. Both flock to this part of the Texas coast in late October and remain until the end of March. Rockport residents welcome the feathered snowbirds with several protected refuges, and the RVers can take their choice of many well-manicured camp-grounds, complete with a friendly small-town atmosphere.

Make your first stop the Rockport-Fulton Area Chamber of Commerce at 404 Broadway. Here you can load up on free brochures and maps, as well as advice from "charmers"—volunteers representing the Charm of the Texas Coast. The chamber also has a handy checklist of fifty-one things to do in the Rockport-Fulton area. A popular activity is a gallery walk of the town's many art galleries.

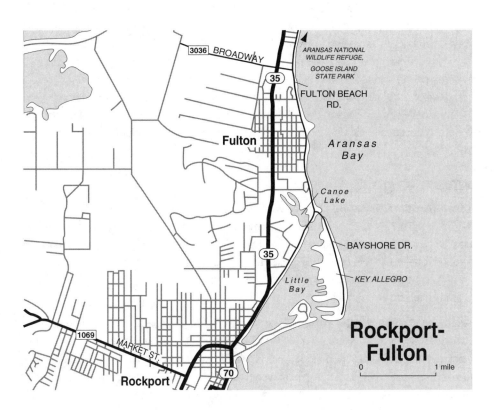

Rockport and neighboring Fulton have quickly caught the attention of the birding world. In the 1940s a feisty and dedicated local amateur bird-watcher named Connie Hagar identified hundreds of species. Her research brought Rockport-Fulton to the attention of the National Wildlife Service and other organizations, which eventually recorded nearly 500 species in the area. Today Rockport-Fulton is renowned as one of the finest birding spots in the world.

The Connie Hagar Sanctuary, downtown along TX 35 at Little Bay, is a good place to spot pelicans and many shorebirds. Whooping cranes winter at the Aransas National Wildlife Refuge northeast of town, and the drive to the refuge passes many marshes and coastal plains filled with birds.

Numerous birds fly through the area during fall and winter migration. Every September, Rockport-Fulton hosts the Hummer/Bird Celebration to mark the passage of thousands of hummingbirds that stop in Rockport-Fulton on their way south to Central and South America. Bird lovers from around the country come to watch this feeding frenzy, when up to 150 hummingbirds often swarm the same feeder. The annual spring migration each May also brings hundreds of colorful songbirds to the area.

Bird-watching opportunities are available year-round. Contact the Rockport-Fulton Area Chamber of Commerce to order a copy of the "Birder's Guide." It illustrates the most common species found here, such as pelicans, cranes, storks, and laughing gulls. It also features driving tours to sixteen birding sites.

Except for year-round boat tours and special bus tours during the Hummer/Bird Celebration, you must depend on self-guided drives to good birding sites. The chamber can give you directions to the best locations outside of town, as well as information about recent spottings.

where to go

Texas Maritime Museum. 1202 Navigation Circle, on downtown waterfront; (866) 729–AHOY or (361) 729–1271; www.texasmaritimemuseum.org. This two-story museum chronicles Texas maritime activities, starting with Spanish shipwrecks off the coast and continuing through today's offshore oil and gas industries. Special exhibits are devoted to shipbuilding, Texans of the sea, the *LaBelle* shipwreck, and fishing. Open Tuesday through Saturday and Sunday afternoons. Fee.

Rockport Center for the Arts. Across the street from Texas Maritime Museum; (361) 729–5519; www.rockportartcenter.org. This restored 1890 house is now the home of the Rockport Art Association and a good place to buy a painting of a Texas beach scene by a local artist. Look for changing exhibits every month. Open Tuesday through Saturday, and Sunday afternoons. Free.

Rockport Beach Park. Downtown, just off TX 35. This is a very popular spot, especially during warm weather. The 1-mile beach offers swimming, picnicking, a children's playground, boating, fishing, and crabbing off an 800-foot pier, as well as paddleboat and Jet Ski rentals. There's also a bird-watching platform overlooking an island said to be the home of one of the best colonies of birds in the state. Open daily. Fee.

Fulton Mansion State Historic Structure. Three miles north of Rockport off TX 35, corner of Henderson Street and Fulton Beach Road; (361) 729–0386; www.tpwd.state.tx.us. Built in 1876 by Col. George Fulton, this grand four-story home overlooks Aransas Bay. It features interesting architecture and surprising modern conveniences. Built at a cost of $100,000, the house included central forced-air heating. A central cast-iron furnace in the basement provided heat through a series of flues to false, decorative fireplaces in the main rooms. Hot and cold running water was achieved with a tank located in the tower attic. A gas plant located at the back of the house provided fuel for gas chandeliers.

Visitors are asked to wear flat, soft-soled shoes because of delicate Axminster and Brussels carpets purchased from New York. Tours of the home's twenty-nine rooms are conducted Wednesday through Sunday. Fee.

***Pisces* Cruises.** Depart from Rockport Harbor; (800) 245–9324 or (361) 729–7525. From November through April, this 58-foot vessel conducts whooping-crane tours daily and twice on Saturday. The remainder of the year, the *Pisces* operates as a party fishing boat, offering daily morning cruises and deep-sea fishing. Fee.

Demo Bird Gardens and Wetlands Pond. Picnic area on east side of TX 35. Stop by this demonstration garden for a look at plants that attract hummingbirds and butterflies. Firecracker bush, cape honeysuckle, Mexican Turk's cap, and lantana are a few of the native plants that help keep Rockport buzzing with winged visitors. Free.

Goose Island State Park. TX 35 and Park Road 13, 21 miles northeast of Rockport; (361) 729–2858; www.tpwd.state.tx.us. This 314-acre park is the home of "the Big Tree," the coastal live oak state champion. The park is also home to a variety of waterfowl and shorebirds. Anglers try for speckled trout, redfish, drum, flounder, and sheepshead. Fee.

Aransas National Wildlife Refuge. (361) 286–3559; www.fws.gov. Forty-five minutes northeast of Rockport. Take TX 35 north to FM 774, turn right, and continue to the intersection of FM 2040. Turn right and stay on FM 2040 to the refuge. This 54,829-acre refuge is the prime wintering ground for the endangered whooping crane, plus hundreds of other bird species. The refuge includes several hiking trails and a paved, 15-mile loop drive that offer a chance to see some of the eighty mammal species indigenous to the region: opossum, shrew, bat, armadillo, raccoon, coati, ringtail, mink, weasel, nutria, skunk, bobcat, white-tailed deer, coyote, and even wild boar.

The observation tower is located on the loop drive. From its heights you can view the elegant whooping cranes, whose numbers once dwindled to only sixteen. Thanks to conservation programs, the present population has increased tenfold. The visitor center includes films and exhibits on the annual migration of these 5-foot-tall birds. Across the road, have a look at native alligators resting in a swampy, fenced enclosure. Open daily. Fee.

Copano Bay Causeway State Fishing Pier. (361) 729–7762. This park is a favorite with anglers, who will find fishing piers and concessions. There's also a public boat launch ramp. Open daily. Fee.

where to eat

The Boiling Pot. Fulton Beach Road; (361) 729–6972. Don a bib, grab a Mamba beer from one of the thirty-one Baskin Robbins–like selections, and sit down. This roadside shack is always noisy, crowded, and fun. The Cajun Combo features blue crab, shrimp, andouille sausage, new potatoes, and corn, all boiled up in a spicy pot and dumped from a metal container onto the paper-covered table. You crack the crab claws with a wooden mallet and dip the succulent flesh in melted butter. Fingers, not forks, are the rule here; dainty eaters need not apply. This is a Texas experience to savor. Open for dinner only from Monday through Thursday; lunch and dinner Friday through Sunday. $–$$.

Sandollar Pavilion. 919 North Fulton Beach Road; (361) 729–2381. This restaurant swears the food here is so fresh that "it slept in the ocean last night." Built over the water, the dining room has a beautiful view of Aransas Bay. Call for hours. Open for breakfast, lunch, and dinner, but closed between meals on some days. $$.

where to stay

Rockport has a huge selection of accommodations, ranging from fishing cottages to elegantly furnished condominiums. Because of the large number of Winter Texans who call Rockport home during the cooler months, many RV and trailer parks and condominiums lease by the day, week, or month. For a brochure listing all of Rockport-Fulton's varied lodgings, call the chamber of commerce office at (800) 242–0071.

Key Allegro Rentals. 1798 Bayshore Drive, just over Key Allegro Bridge on Fulton Beach Road; (800) 348–1627 or (361) 729–3691; www.keyallegro.com. Key Allegro is a small island linked to Rockport by an arched bridge. The lovely drive here is your first hint at the elegant accommodations awaiting visitors in this area. Nicely appointed condominium units and upscale homes located on the water's edge afford beautiful views of Rockport's fishing vessels heading out for the day's catch. Rental homes and condominiums are available by the day or week. $$–$$$.

connie hagar

The eyes (and binoculars) of the birding world were focused on Rockport due to the efforts of the late Connie Hagar, a woman who became somewhat of a legend along the Coastal Bend. She, herself, migrated to Rockport in the 1930s, drawn because of the large number of birds she had seen on an earlier visit.

For more than three decades she chronicled the comings and goings of hundreds of species. Connie Hagar was not an ornithologist, but a birder who enjoyed the feathered visitors. Today, you can visit the Connie Hagar Bird Sanctuary in downtown Rockport, a marshy grassland that is a stopping place for many sea birds, not to mention the many birders who sit on the piers and revel at the magnificent great blue herons and pelicans.

Laguna Reef Condos and Hotel. 1021 Water Street; (800) 248–1057 or (361) 729–1742. This waterfront hotel and condominium resort has an unbeatable view of the bay, especially for early risers who want to watch the gorgeous sunrise. Each fully furnished unit has a private balcony, kitchen, and dining/living room. After a day of sightseeing, take a walk along the complex's beach or down the long fishing pier. The units rent by the day, week, or month. $$.

Kontiki Beach Motel and Condominiums. Fulton Beach Road; (800) 242–3407. The motel offers spacious accommodations that feature a living and dining area, fully equipped kitchen, and separate bedroom, available by the day, week, or month. Guests also can rent nicely furnished condominiums. All take in a view of the water. Prices vary.

especially for winter texans

Rockport hosts many special events for Winter Texans, from fishing to horseshoe tournaments. The town sponsors several Winter Texan arts and crafts shows, as well as concerts played by talented seasonal residents.

The Paws and Taws Center on Fulton Beach Road is the site of many gatherings for the winter visitors who stay in Rockport and Fulton. With a hardwood floor, a stage, and kitchen facilities, the center holds weekly square dances, bingo games, AARP meetings, and State Days, with parties for visitors from specific states.

Fulton sponsors an annual Welcome Winter Texans free fish fry in early December. The Rockport area includes many excellent RV parks, with busy clubhouse activities. For more information call the Rockport-Fulton Area Chamber of Commerce at (800) 242–0071.

day trip 02

south

coast and cattle:
three rivers, mathis, corpus christi,
padre and mustang islands,
kingsville

three rivers

Located halfway between San Antonio and Corpus Christi on I–37, the community of Three Rivers is best known as the gateway to Choke Canyon.

where to go

Choke Canyon State Park, South Shore Unit. Three and a half miles west of Three Rivers on TX 72; (361) 786–3538; www.tpwd.state.tx.us. This 385-acre park offers visitors camping, boating, hiking, birding, a swimming pool, and many recreation areas. This park and the nearby Calliham Unit comprise Choke Canyon, parks that rest on the banks of the extensive reservoir that supplies water to the city of Corpus Christi. The parks are filled with wildlife, ranging from the Rio Grande turkey to the fox to the American alligator. Open daily. Fee.

Choke Canyon State Park, Calliham Unit. Twelve miles west of Three Rivers on TX 72 to Tilden; (361) 786–3868; www.tpwd.state.tx.us. The larger of the two Choke Canyon parks, this facility sprawls for 1,100 acres. Park facilities include screened shelters, campsites, a sports complex, a swimming pool, tennis, basketball, a birding blind, and more. Open daily. Fee.

mathis

This agricultural capital is located south of San Antonio and is a popular stop for visitors wishing to boat or fish at Lake Corpus Christi State Park. To reach Mathis, drive south on I–37. The city is located just 22 miles from Corpus Christi.

where to go

Lake Corpus Christi State Park. FM 1068, 4 miles southwest of Mathis, off TX 359; (361) 547–2635; www.tpwd.state.tx.us. This sprawling park surrounds the 21,000-acre Lake Corpus Christi, a favorite with boaters and anglers. Activities here include waterskiing, fishing, swimming, hiking, and birding. Open daily. Fee.

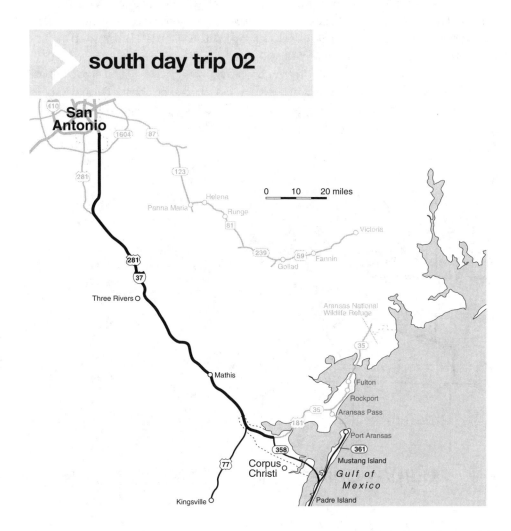

south day trip 02

Lipantitlan State Historical Park. (361) 547–2635; www.tpwd.state.tx.us. South on TX 359 for 31 miles to Orange Grove. Turn east and continue 9 miles on FM 624 and FM 70. This historic park highlights an adobe fort built by the Mexican government in 1833. Today visitors find few facilities here. Open daily. Free.

corpus christi

Continue south on I-37 to Corpus Christi. This city of 278,000 residents is a popular year-round destination. During the summer months, the nearby beaches of Padre and Mustang Islands appeal to surfers, families, and sun worshippers. During the winter, this coastal city fills with Winter Texans.

The waters of Corpus Christi Bay are calm, protected from the Gulf of Mexico by the barrier islands of Padre and Mustang, which served as pirate hideouts even after the area was charted in 1519 by Spanish explorer Alonzo Alvarez de Pineda. He bestowed the bay with its name, which means "body of Christ."

Today Corpus Christi is a thriving city, consistently ranking as one of America's busiest ports. The bayfront is a combination fishing village and tourist spot, and the downtown piers are lined with picturesque shrimp boats. High-rise luxury hotels, specialty shops, and seafood restaurants overlook the bay. The heart of Corpus Christi is Shoreline Boulevard,

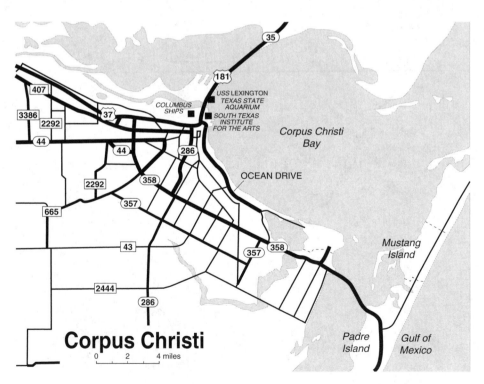

with its proud palms and spectacular views of the water. The handsome boulevard begins as Ocean Drive at the gates of the U.S. Naval Air Station and winds north past grand mansions perched on the bluffs overlooking the bay.

Because of the warm weather and a fairly consistent breeze of about 12 miles per hour, Corpus Christi is known as the unofficial windsurfing capital of the United States, site of the U.S. Open Windsurfing Regatta. It's not unusual to see the bay dotted with the colorful sails. Ocean Drive's Oleander Park is the only city-sanctioned sailboard park in the world. If you want to give the sport a try, several operators along South Padre Island Drive offer instruction and rentals.

The north section of Shoreline Boulevard contains the huge piers known as Coopers Street L-Head, Lawrence Street T-Head, and Peoples Street T-Head. Each pier bustles with life, from the predawn hours when the shrimp boats leave until midnight; the night cruises offer anglers a chance at trophy tarpon, kingfish, or marlin. Peoples Street T-Head is also home of the *Flagship,* an 85-foot paddle wheeler that offers guided bay tours. The northern end of Shoreline Boulevard also holds the Art Museum of South Texas, the World of Discovery: Museum of Science and History, and the Ships of Christopher Columbus. At the end of the drive is the Harbor Bridge. Built in 1959 to link the city with the small towns that line the Texas coast, it leads across the ship channel to the Texas State Aquarium.

Many music fans make a special stop at the Selena Memorial, a privately erected statue that remembers the Tejano star who was killed in 1995. The statue is located on the downtown seawall at Mirador del Flor. The seawall is always a popular spot with in-line skaters, cyclists, and couples who come to stroll the promenade.

where to go

Texas State Aquarium. 2710 Shoreline Drive, across ship channel from the downtown area; (800) 477–GULF; www.texasstateaquarium.org. The Texas State Aquarium focuses on sea life of the Gulf of Mexico, the first such facility in the nation. The Gulf of Mexico Exhibit Building, a $31.5 million facility, houses 250 species, including grouper, eels, and sharks.

This must-see attraction showcases the aquatic animals and habitats indigenous to the Gulf of Mexico. You'll enter the interpretive center beneath a cascading waterfall, symbolic of the dive into coastal waters. It's a self-guided discovery through exhibits such as the Islands of Steel, a look at a replica of an offshore oil platform surrounded by nurse sharks, amberjack, and other marine creatures commonly found around these man-made reefs. Nearby, the Flower Gardens Coral Reef exhibit looks at the beautiful coral gardens found 115 miles off the coast, blooming with aquatic life and marine animals such as moray eels, tarpon, and rays. Outdoors, young visitors enjoy touch tanks filled with small sharks and rays; the Otter Space, where playful river otters amuse visitors with their antics; and the Octopus' Garden, a 20-foot-tall purple octopus playscape that invites young visitors to enjoy the marine-inspired playground.

High-tech displays feature the use of a video monitor to help you guide the image of an underwater robotic arm. Touch-screen monitors offer a chance for visitors to try their hand at environmental decision making. When you're finished here, walk outside for a look at the ship channel, the Harbor Bridge, and an unbeatable view of the city. Open daily. Fee.

Dolphin Connection. Beneath US 181 bridge to Portland, just before Nueces Bay Causeway. Two Dolphin Connection boats take visitors into the bay to feed and interact with dolphins. Owners Erv and Sonja Strong know the wild mammals by name and are glad to explain their habits, family connections, and lifestyle. You can hand feed and pet these remarkable creatures during the hour-long excursion. Open daily from March through October or November, when the dolphins leave for the winter. Fee. For reservations call (361) 776–2887 or write 215 Bridgeport Avenue, Suite 4, Corpus Christi, TX 78402.

South Texas Institute for the Arts. 1902 North Shoreline Boulevard, Bayfront Arts and Science Park; (361) 825–3500; www.stia.org. Famous for its stark white architecture, this museum is filled with changing fine-art exhibits of traditional and contemporary works. Open Tuesday through Sunday. Fee.

Watergardens. Bayfront Arts and Science Park; no phone. A man-made stream tumbles from the entrance of the art museum down to a sunken circle of flags and fountains. This is a nice place to take a box lunch. Open daily. Free.

Museum of Science and History. 1900 North Chaparral, Bayfront Arts and Science Park; (361) 826–4650; www.ccmuseum.com. This museum is filled with natural history exhibits, including displays recalling the many Spanish shipwrecks found off the Gulf Coast. Children can climb aboard a re-creation of a fifteenth-century vessel for a peek at the cramped quarters endured by early explorers.

Don't miss the exhibit, designed by the Smithsonian's National Museum of Natural History for the 500th anniversary of the European discovery of America.

After a look at exhibits that tell the story of these explorers and the effects their arrival had on the New World, see for yourself what it was like to make the Atlantic crossing aboard the *Niña, Pinta,* and *Santa Maria*. Life-size replicas of these Spanish ships are located in a shipyard repair facility adjacent to the museum.

These re-creations of the Columbus fleet were built by the Spanish government at the cost of more than $7 million to commemorate the 500th anniversary of the explorer's voyage. You can board the *Pinta* and the *Santa Maria;* onshore exhibits explain more about sea travel and the Spanish voyages. Open Tuesday through Sunday. Fee.

Captain Clark *Flagship* Cruises. Peoples Street T-Head; (361) 884–1693; www.capt clarksflagship.com. Several daily tours take visitors for a look at the shipyards and the bay. Sunset cruises are particularly scenic, with the lights of downtown reflected in the calm bay waters. Closed Tuesday. Fee.

Corpus Christi Botanical Gardens. 8545 South Staples Drive; (361) 852–2100; www .ccbotanicalgardens.org. Take South Staples Drive toward Kingsville, past Oso Creek; signs mark entrance. These gardens feature native South Texas plants and winding trails through subtropical foliage. Open Tuesday through Sunday. Fee.

USS *Lexington* Museum on the Bay. (800) LADY–LEX; www.usslexington.com. This aircraft carrier is berthed just offshore from the Texas State Aquarium, and visitors have permission to come aboard. Sunk four times in World War II, the ship returned to fight again. Today this carrier, with a main deck larger than three football fields, is a museum open daily for tours. Texas's first flight simulator takes up to sixteen passengers on a three- to five-minute flight. Hydraulically powered, the "cabin" uses a combination of sight, sound, and movement to give passengers the sensation of riding in either an attack airplane or a helicopter. Fee.

Texas State Museum of Asian Cultures. 1809 North Chaparral; (361) 882–2641. This museum focuses on all aspects of Asian arts. Open Tuesday through Saturday. Fee.

Heritage Park. 1581 North Chaparral; (361) 883–0639; www.ccparkandrec.com. Located a short walk from the convention center, this park contains numerous historic homes relocated here from around the region. Tours are available at 10:30 A.M. Thursday and Friday for homes that date from the mid-nineteenth century. Open weekdays. Free (fee for tours).

where to eat

Landry's Dockside. Peoples Street T-Head; (361) 882–6666. This restaurant is a restored two-story barge that sports a casual, fun atmosphere. Murals of fish span the walls, and huge picture windows offer a great view. The specialty of the house is Gulf seafood, including shrimp, oysters, and scallops. Open for lunch and dinner daily. $$.

Water Street Seafood Company and Water Street Oyster Bar. 309 North Water Street, Water Street Market; (361) 881–9448. Located just a block from Shoreline Boulevard, this casual restaurant features Cajun-inspired seafood as well as the usual Gulf Coast fare. Open daily for lunch and dinner. $$–$$$.

Elmo's City Diner. 622 North Water Street; (361) 883–1643. This fun restaurant boasts a 1950s diner atmosphere. The menu includes all types of American dishes from chicken to burgers, as well as fresh Gulf seafood. $$–$$$.

where to stay

Omni Corpus Christi Bayfront. 900 North Shoreline Boulevard; (800) THE–OMNI or (361) 887–1600; www.omnihotels.com. This elegant 474-room hotel overlooks the bay and includes a health club, swimming pool, and rooftop dining room. Many of Corpus Christi's main attractions lie within walking distance. $$$.

Embassy Suites Hotel. 4337 South Padre Island Drive; (800) EMBASSY or (361) 853–7899; www.embassysuites.com. This all-suite hotel is located on the north side of town, fifteen minutes from Shoreline Boulevard and Padre Island. The huge open lobby and atrium include a heated pool, hot tub, and sauna, as well as a dining area that serves a free all-you-can-eat breakfast plus evening cocktails. $$.

Holiday Inn Emerald Beach. 1102 South Shoreline Boulevard; (361) 883–5731; www.ichotelsgroup.com. The only hotel in downtown Corpus Christi with a beach (albeit a small one), this property is very popular with families. The 368-room hotel includes a restaurant, a pool, an exercise room, a game room, and a playground. $$–$$$.

Omni Corpus Christi Marina. 707 North Shoreline Boulevard; (800) THE–OMNI or (361) 882–1600; www.omnihotels.com. This bayfront hotel offers 346 guest rooms, a pool, a restaurant, and more. The location, like its sister property the Omni Corpus Christi Bayfront, is excellent for anyone wanting to be right in the heart of downtown. $$$.

Sea Shell Inn. 202 Kleberg Place; (361) 888–5391. Located on Corpus Christi Beach at the base of the Harbor Bridge, this twenty-six-room property includes many rooms with kitchenettes. The hotel includes beach access and a pool. $–$$.

padre and mustang islands

To reach the islands, head out on South Padre Island Drive, also called TX 358. The road is lined with shell shops, windsurfing rentals, bait stands, and car washes. In the shallow waters along the drive, many anglers stand waist deep in salt water alongside tall herons and pelicans looking for a meal.

When you cross the Intracoastal Waterway via the enormous JFK Causeway Bridge, you leave the mainland for Padre Island. This 110-mile barrier island protects much of the Texas coast from hurricanes and tropical storms. Generally, the northern stretch of island paralleling the area from Corpus Christi to Port Mansfield is called Padre Island; from that point to the tip of Texas, the land mass is named South Padre Island.

Padre and Mustang Islands feature beaches dotted with rolling dunes, clean sand, and flocks of gulls. The surf is usually gentle and shallow enough to walk for hundreds of yards before reaching chest-deep water. Occasionally undertow is a problem, but on most summer days the waves are gentle and rolling, and the water is warm.

To reach the Padre Island beaches, continue straight on South Padre Island Drive (Park Road 22). Visitors can choose from several parks here, each with its own special charm. One of these, the Padre Balli Park, is named for the priest who managed a ranch on the island in the early nineteenth century. It offers a 1,200-foot fishing pier. The Padre Island National Seashore has a snack bar, and showers are available at Malaquite Beach. Although vehicles are allowed on most Padre beaches, Malaquite is one where vehicles are not permitted.

Beyond Malaquite lies 66 miles of protected beach in Padre Island National Seashore, accessible only by four-wheel-drive vehicles. Little Shell and Big Shell Beaches are located in this area.

Although much of Padre Island is undeveloped, you'll find many commercial establishments on neighboring Mustang Island. To reach it, turn left off South Padre Island Drive from Corpus Christi onto Park Road 53. Only 18 miles long, Mustang Island is far smaller than its neighbor to the south, but it shares many of the same attractions. One of the best stops is Mustang Island State Park (361–749–5246), where showers, restrooms, and camping are available. Cars, however, are prohibited on the beach.

Whether you choose Mustang or Padre, follow a few rules of safety. Portuguese man-of-war jellyfish are commonly seen on the beaches. If you are stung, locals claim the best relief is a paste of meat tenderizer and water applied to the bite. A far less dangerous, but very annoying, aspect of the Gulf beaches are tar balls. These black clumps, formed by natural seepage and offshore oil spills, wash up on the beach and stick to your skin and your shoes. Many hotels have a tar removal station near the door to help you remove the sticky substance.

where to go

Mustang Island State Park. Park Road 53; (361) 749–5246; www.tpwd.state.tx.us. Mustang Island State Park is clean and enjoyable, perfect for a weekend of RV or tent camping or just a few hours of beachcombing. Freshwater showers are available. Covered picnic tables help keep your gear out of the sand. Open daily. Fee.

where to stay

Holiday Inn North Padre Island. 15202 Windward Drive; (888) 949–8041 or (361) 949–8041; www.holiday-inn.com. Here you can walk from the hotel directly to the beach. When you've had enough salt water, have a dip in the hotel swimming pool. $$.

Island House. 15340 Leeward Drive, Padre Island; (800) 333–8806. This beachfront condominium resort has well-furnished units, many with beautiful views of the Gulf. Each includes a furnished kitchen, a dining/living room, and two bedrooms. Spend the extra money for an oceanfront condo, with sliding glass doors in the living room and the master bedroom. $$$.

Gulfstream. 14810 Windward Drive; (800) 542–7368 or (361) 949–8061. This 132-room property includes a pool, a game room, and more. $$$.

kingsville

Perhaps no other destination quite epitomizes "Texas size" like the King Ranch. Larger than the state of Rhode Island, the King Ranch sprawls across 825,000 acres and, even more importantly, stands as a symbol of Texas ingenuity. The ranch has long been known for its role in the American ranching industry and is still a worldwide leader. Many of the practices used industrywide started here.

The ranch is located on the outskirts of Kingsville, 39 miles south of Corpus Christi on US 77. The Kingsville Visitor Center is at the intersection of US 77 and Corral Drive and makes a good stop to pick up area brochures and maps.

Just a few blocks away, the historic downtown is included on the National Register of Historic Places. Kleberg Avenue and King Street are lined with antiques shops and specialty stores.

But the prime attraction in this community is the King Ranch, located 39 miles south of Corpus Christi. Visitors can enjoy a guided tour of the ranch in air-conditioned buses. Don't expect reenactments of typical ranch activities here, though—this is the real thing. Cowboys, more often seen riding pickup trucks than horses, work more than 60,000 head of cattle on this ranch.

The King Ranch also offers nature trails that provide glimpses of white-tailed deer, javelinas, coyotes, and other animals native to this region, first known as the Wild Horse Desert.

King Ranch traces its history to 1853, when it was founded by Capt. Richard King, a self-made man who left home at an early age and made his fortune on Rio Grande river-boats. The ranch, still one of the largest in the world, developed the Santa Gertrudis and King Ranch Santa Cruz breeds of cattle (the only two registered breeds developed in the United States), as well as the first registered American quarter horse.

Many fall and winter visitors also come to enjoy a look at the feathered residents and migratory birds. A stop on the Coastal Birding Trail, the ranch is home to more than 300 feathered species. Species such as green jays, pygmy owls, and common paurauque are spotted on different areas of the ranch.

where to go

Conner Museum. Santa Gertrudis Street on the campus of Texas A&M University; (361) 593–2810. Highlighting the natural and social history of South Texas, the museum includes exhibits on ranching, South Texas ecosystems, and area fossil and minerals. Open Monday through Saturday. Free.

King Ranch Visitor Center. TX 141 West; (361) 592–8055; www.king-ranch.com. The center is a gathering place for tours of the King Ranch. A continuously running film about the history of the ranch gives guests an overview of the operation. Visitors also sign up for guided one-and-a-half-hour tours (call for tour times). The guided bus tours begin at the site where Captain King first camped in 1852 and continue to cover both the history and the modern workings of the ranch. Special-interest tours of cattle operations, feedlots, and other aspects of the ranch are available by appointment. Nature tours, including special programs for birders, are scheduled several times annually. Open daily (afternoons only on Sunday). Free (except for tours).

King Ranch Museum. 405 North Sixth Street; (361) 595–1881; www.king-ranch.com. Beyond the ranch in the town of Kingsville, the King legacy is also apparent. The museum provides visitors with a look at the history of the ranch, including a stunning photographic essay of life on King Ranch in the 1940s. A collection of saddles, antique carriages, and antique cars rounds out the exhibits. Open 10:00 A.M. to 4:00 P.M. weekdays, afternoons only on weekends. Fee.

where to shop

King Ranch Saddle Shop. 201 East Kleberg Avenue; (800) 282–KING; www.krsaddle shop.com. Just down the street from the King Ranch Museum, the saddle shop carries on the tradition of saddle making that began after the Civil War when Captain King started his own saddle shop. It produces fine purses, belts, and saddles in downtown Kingsville's John B. Ragland Mercantile Company Building. Open Monday through Saturday.

Sellers Market. 205 East Kleberg; (361) 595–4992. Handmade arts and crafts fill this marketplace. Open Tuesday through Saturday.

captain king

King Ranch traces its history to 1853, when it was founded by Capt. Richard King, who made his fortune on Rio Grande riverboats.

This area that was first called the Wild Horse Desert by early settlers and later became part of the Rincon de Santa Gertrudis Spanish Land Grant was tamed by Captain King. King first saw the land when traveling from Brownsville to Corpus Christi to attend the Lone Star Fair. He traveled 124 miles north of Brownsville before reaching what must have seemed like an oasis: the mesquite-shaded Santa Gertrudis Creek. Soon he and his friend Texas Ranger Capt. Gideon K. "Legs" Lewis set about forming a partnership, a livestock operation headquartered at this creek.

In the coming years, King fenced these rugged coastal plains and moved an entire village from Mexico to staff the ranch, people who would become the first cowboys of Texas.

where to eat

Wild Olive Cafe. 205 East Kleberg; (361) 595–4992. Located in the Sellers Market, this volunteer-operated cafe offers a taste of Kingsville with homemade lunches served by volunteers every Wednesday through Friday. $.

where to stay

Rodeway Inn Kingsville. 3430 South US 77; (361) 595–5753. Located just minutes from downtown, this family-style hotel includes a restaurant and outdoor pool. $$.

southwest

day trip 01

southwest

run for the border:
devine; pearsall; dilley; cotulla;
laredo; nuevo laredo, mexico

The 153-mile drive from San Antonio to Laredo via I–35 is a fast one. Although a few small towns appear on this stretch, much of the area remains ranch land.

devine

Just 32 miles outside of San Antonio on I–35 lies Devine, a community that was founded as a railroad station in 1881. Named for a San Antonio judge, Devine is a quiet town that's best known as an agricultural center. Six miles southeast of the town lies the smaller community of Bigfoot, named for Texas Ranger Bigfoot Wallace, who took part in the Texas War of Independence.

pearsall

Continue down I–35 for 22 miles to the community of Pearsall. This home of just fewer than 8,000 residents is the capital of the region's peanut crop (there's even a peanut monument downtown).

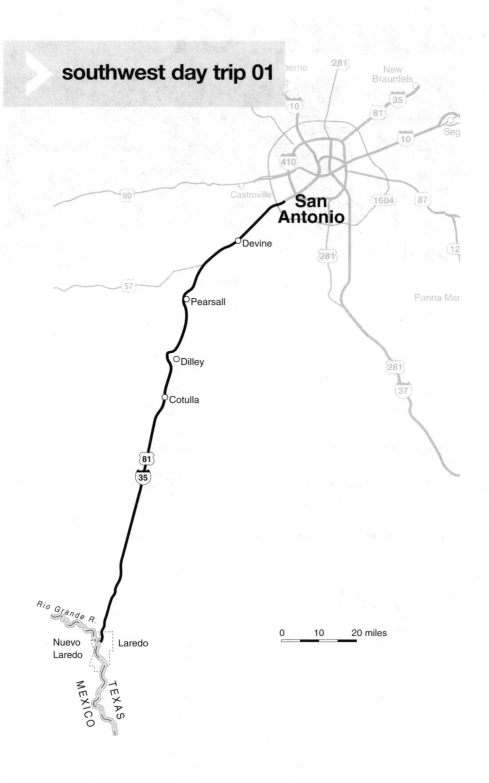

southwest day trip 01

where to go

Old Frio County Jail Museum. Cedar and Medina Streets; (830) 334–9414 (chamber of commerce). This former jail is now filled with local-history artifacts recounting the town's early days as a railroad community. Open Tuesday through Saturday. Free.

dilley

Drive south on I–35 for 17 miles to the community of Dilley, also known for its agriculture. Although peanuts are also grown in this region, here watermelons are king. Dilley's economy also has benefited from another benefactor: oil.

Many visitors have another reason to visit this community of just 3,000 residents. With more than 250 species spotted, Dilley is known for its birding.

where to go

Dilley Chamber of Commerce. Miller and Main Streets; (830) 334–9414. Stop by this office for free information on local attractions and activities.

Watermelon Statue. City Park on Main Street. Truly a Texas-size watermelon, this statue is Dilley's favorite photo spot. The statue is located in City Park, which includes picnic tables. Open daily. Free.

where to eat

Pancho Garcia Cafe Restaurant. I–35 and TX 117; (830) 965–1493. This diner, popular with bus groups on their way to the border, serves breakfast, lunch, and dinner. Tex-Mex specialties are popular, along with steaks, quail, and catfish. $–$$.

cotulla

Located 16 miles south of Dilley, Cotulla has been home to several notable residents, including Lyndon Baines Johnson and short-story author William Sidney Porter, better known as O. Henry. The town of just fewer than 5,000 residents is a center for the area's cattle and sheep ranching industries.

where to go

Brush Country Museum. 201 South Stewart Street; (830) 879–2326 (chamber of commerce). This museum, housed in the school where Lyndon Baines Johnson once taught, features local-history exhibits. Open Tuesday and Thursday from 10:00 A.M. to noon and 2:00 to 4:00 P.M., Wednesday, Friday, and Saturday from 1:00 to 4:00 P.M. Free.

laredo

Continue 68 miles south on I–35 to the city of Laredo. This city has long been known as the South Texas party spot. It's a popular weekend trip with college students, shoppers, and anyone in search of fun. Built on the banks of the Rio Grande, Laredo dates from 1755. Founded by an officer of the Royal Army of Spain, it was one of the first cities established in this part of the country.

Following the war with Mexico, many Laredo residents packed up and headed across the border to start their own city in Mexico. They named the fledgling community Nuevo Laredo or "New Laredo." Healthy trade between the United States and Mexico along with the fact that many families straddle both sides of the border have linked the cities. Thus the nickname Los Dos Laredos—The Two Laredos.

To reach Laredo's downtown district, take the last exit off I–35 and drive along a narrow, one-way avenue called Zaragoza Street. With its old buildings, constant traffic, and stately palms, the venue has a definite Mexican feel. Wholesalers along Zaragoza Street entice shoppers with goods, including electronics, clothing, shoes, jewelry, and perfumes.

On the right is the enormous San Agustin Church, founded in 1778. The church overlooks the San Agustin Plaza, a popular place just to sit and watch the flurry of activity near the bridge. This plaza, with its peaceful gazebo and gas-powered lamps, was the site of one of the West's bloodiest shootouts. In 1886 the *Botas* (boots) and *Huaraches* (sandals), two rival political groups, battled here, leaving more than eighty dead when the smoke cleared.

Beyond the city streets lies a whole other side of Laredo—a place filled with desert wildlife, walking trails, fish-filled lakes, and more. Birders find more than 300 species on record in the brush country, including several rare species. Anglers find plenty of challenge at Lake Casa Blanca, filled with black bass as well as blue and yellow catfish. Not far from the lake lies the Casa Blanca Lake Golf Course, an eighteen-hole challenge that you can play year-round. And don't forget your walking shoes. Texas A&M International University and Laredo Community College have designated walking trails in the area that take in riverfront property as well as brush country.

Always boasting a fiesta spirit, the city of Laredo and its sister city, Nuevo Laredo, really swing into gear at a time of year when many communities are caught in a festival lull. February marks a time of fun for all ages in this border city.

When February rolls around, this city really puts on its party hat—birthday party hat, that is. The guest of honor is George Washington, and in the sister cities of Laredo and Nuevo Laredo, his birthday is not just a holiday, it's a full-blown fiesta. For nearly two weeks, the cities are filled with every kind of festival activity imaginable. Billed as the largest observance of George Washington's birthday in the nation, the event draws close to 400,000 partygoers.

For more than a century, the towns have celebrated every February with the George Washington birthday celebration as a way to spread international goodwill between the

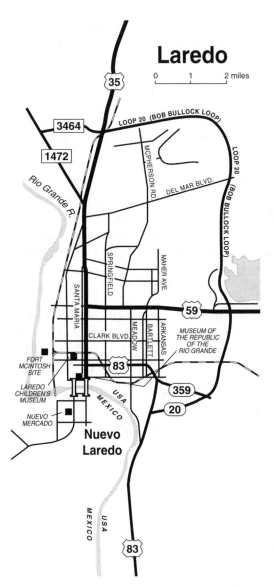

neighboring countries. A Laredo men's organization, the Red Men and the White Men, holds a mock battle representing a fight for possession of the city, one that culminates in an unconditional surrender when the mayor gives the key to the city to Great Chief Sachem.

How does this relate to George Washington? The American leader was named Sachem by the Sons of Liberty when they disguised themselves as Indians during their battle for freedom. Because of this, the Laredo organization picked the first president's birthday as the occasion for the remembrance of this event.

Today George Washington's birthday has grown into South Texas's largest event, with activities for every age group. Sporting events, a children's carnival, dances, parades, and gala balls fill the entire month with revelry. Events include the WBCA Carnival, popular with families.

George Washington's birthday is known for its fun, food, and fireworks, but it's also noted because of its elegant balls. The Princess Pocahontas Pageant and Ball features Laredo debutantes wearing Native American regalia, gowns that take as long as two years to research and prepare. The Society of Martha Washington Colonial Pageant and Ball, one of the largest social events in South Texas, draws many spectators.

The days of activities come to a hot climax with the Jalapeño Festival, held during the final days of the bash. Events range from a "Jello"peño-eating contest to a jalapeño pizza–eating contest to the popular International Waiters Race, where waiters from both sides of the border race a course while balancing a tray with a bottle of champagne and a set of glasses.

Whether you visit Laredo during the GWB celebration or any time of the year, you'll find a festive atmosphere in this border community. A favorite stop for Texas bargain hunters, Laredo and nearby Nuevo Laredo act as a magnet for the dedicated shopper.

where to go

Texas Travel Information Center. I–35 North at exit 18. This facility offers Texas information, maps, and brochures for locations across Texas. Picnic facilities are available on the grounds.

Museum of the Republic of the Rio Grande. 1003 Zaragoza Street, adjacent to the La Posada Hotel; (956) 727–3480. Six flags have flown over most of Texas, but Laredo has seen seven, thanks to the short-lived Republic of the Rio Grande. This museum is housed in a one-story adobe structure that was once the capitol building of the latter republic, a country formed when northern Mexico seceded from Mexico in 1839. The new state existed until 1841. The museum contains guns, saddles, and household belongings from that brief period. Open Tuesday through Sunday. Fee.

Laredo Children's Museum. West end of Washington Street at Fort MacIntosh; (956) 728–0404; www.laredochildrensmuseum.org. Kids enjoy touching and manipulating the exhibits at this hands-on museum. Children can even stand inside a bubble in one exhibit. Fee.

Walking Tour of Laredo. The streets of Laredo are lined with historic structures, including many old churches and homes built in the Mexican vernacular and Victorian styles. Walking tours are provided by the Webb County Heritage Foundation at 500 Flores Avenue. For more information call (956) 727–0977. Fee.

La Casa Blanca International State Park. Five miles east off US 59 on Loop 20; (956) 725–3826. This park offers picnic facilities, hiking trails, and a playground. Open daily. Fee.

San Agustin Church. 214 San Agustin Avenue. This historic church was the site of the bloody shootout in 1886. Open daily. Free.

where to shop

San Bernardo Avenue. If you don't want to drive into Mexico, you'll find many large importers on this shopping strip. Wrought-iron furniture, clay products, and vases are popular buys.

Zaragoza Street Wholesalers. When Mexicans come into Texas to shop, many make this strip their first stop. Shops here sell the same merchandise, from handbags to headsets, found at many department stores, but at bargain prices. Shops are located throughout the historic district north of Zaragoza Street.

Vegas's Imports. 4002 San Bernardo; (956) 724–8251. Mexican home furnishings for every room of the house are sold in this well-stocked store, and much of the furniture is hand carved.

Polly Adams. 101 Calle del Norte; (956) 723–2969. For nearly four decades, this upscale store has offered exclusive lines of women's clothing and accessories. Formerly housed in Mall del Norte, the shop relocated to this sprawling store, which spans more than 7,000 square feet. The customer-oriented shop includes large fitting rooms with dressing robes, a living room so customers can take a break from their shopping to visit, and complimentary coffee, tea, and wine. Frequented by many Mexican movie stars as well as discerning shoppers from around Texas, Polly Adams can provide meals for shoppers with advance notice and always has several seamstresses on hand to provide a personalized fit.

where to eat

Tack Room Bar and Grill. 1000 Zaragoza Street at La Posada Hotel; (800) 444–2099 or (956) 722–1701. This casual restaurant features nightly entertainment and steak and seafood. The upstairs restaurant offers candlelight dining, an exhibition kitchen and grill, and a romantic atmosphere. The building originally housed Laredo's first telephone exchange. $$$.

where to stay

La Posada. 1000 Zaragoza Street; (800) 444–2099 or (956) 722–1701; www.laposada hotel.com. This 224-room hotel is the closest accommodation to the International Bridge leading from Laredo into Mexico. Two Spanish-style courtyards feature tall palms, blooming bougainvillaea, and refreshing pools, one with a swim-up bar. A relaxed lobby restaurant specializes in Mexican dishes while two elegant restaurants specialize in steak and continental fare. $$$.

Courtyard by Marriott. 2410 Santa Ursula; (956) 725–5555; www.marriott.com. This property includes a restaurant and bar as well as a swimming pool and exercise equipment. $$.

nuevo laredo, mexico

Visitors can cross the border into Mexico by car or on foot (the more popular choice). There's no problem driving across at either International Bridge No. 1, also known as the Old Bridge, or International Bridge No. 2, the I-35 bridge. Trucks now cross outside the city limits.

Nuevo Laredo, with more than 500,000 inhabitants, is far larger than its American sister. The city engages in an enormous import-export business and holds the title as the largest port of entry on the Mexico-U.S. border.

Before leaving Laredo, drivers should invest in short-term Mexican auto insurance. A company carrying this coverage is Sanborn's U.S.-Mexico Insurance Service at 2212 Santa Ursula (956–723–3657). Be sure to read "Entering Mexico," Appendix A, for details on Mexican insurance, proof of citizenship, and prohibited goods.

Most vacationers make the five-minute walk across International Bridge No. 1 to get a better view of the Rio Grande below. You can park your car at the Riverdrive Mall (1600 Water Street) and walk to the Old Bridge. After paying a toll (35 cents) at the entrance to the bridge, you can walk into Mexico. In the middle of the bridge is a plaque that marks the border between the two countries.

Cross over the bridge to the shopping district and Avenida Guerrero, where street vendors hawk everything from chewing gum and paper flowers to tablecloths and strands of garlic. In the downtown area, every road parallel to Guerrero is an avenue, or *avenida;* a road running perpendicular to the avenues (and parallel to the river) is a street, or *calle.*

To call Nuevo Laredo telephone numbers from the United States, first dial the international code (011), then the country code (52), followed by the phone number.

where to go

Turf Club. Calle Bravo and Avenida Ocampo, a few blocks from Nuevo Mercado; (876) 12–0494. This air-conditioned club has live off-track betting, plus a restaurant and bar on the premises. Open daily.

where to shop

Nuevo Mercado. Avenida Guerrero, 4 blocks from the International Bridge. The *mercado,* or market, is the one place that all tourists visit. Here you find many American faces, English-speaking shopkeepers, and a very friendly atmosphere.

Built around two open courtyards filled with umbrella-shaded tables, the two-story market sells just about every imaginable Mexican-made product. Frozen margaritas and Corona beer are in evidence everywhere, offering a chance to cool down after several hours in the stores. Most shops have no air-conditioning, even though summer days often top one hundred degrees. Open daily.

Marti's. Avenida Guerrero, 3 blocks past the International Bridge; (876) 12–3337. This upscale, air-conditioned shop is the nicest store in Nuevo Laredo and the priciest. You don't get a chance to bargain here, so be content with the fact that you're buying the finest jewelry, furnishings, and clothing that Nuevo Laredo has to offer. This place is a favorite with both wealthy Mexicans and South Texas shoppers looking for something above the usual mercado fare. Open daily.

> ## border crime
>
> *At press time, Nuevo Laredo was experiencing a severe crime wave caused by drug cartels. During 2005, nearly 200 murders were reported, including numerous police officers and the police chief; kidnapping was also a problem. The U.S. Consulate's office in Nuevo Laredo closed for a week but has since reopened. Visitors can check with the U.S. Department of State Web site, www.travel.state .gov, for any current news on safety.*

El Cid Glass Factory. Avenida Reforma 3861; (876) 15–8679. This glass factory is one of Nuevo Laredo's shopping treasures, located more than a mile beyond the mercado. You'll want to take a taxi here and then allow plenty of time to shop for blue-, green-, and red-rimmed glasses, bowls, Christmas ornaments, and more. This is Nuevo Laredo's only glass factory, operated by Romualdo Canales for more than twenty years. Open daily.

where to eat

El Dorado (formerly the Cadillac Bar). Calle Belden and Avenida Ocampo, about 2 blocks from Nuevo Mercado; (876) 12–0015. For some travelers, the El Dorado is reason enough to come to Nuevo Laredo. The favorite watering hole for many South Texans, it's the home of the Ramos Gin Fizz, a concoction of gin, lemon juice, and powdered sugar. The menu includes frog's legs and red snapper. $$.

La Principal. Avenida Guerrero 630; (876) 12–1301. Just a few blocks beyond the mercado, this restaurant is a favorite with Nuevo Laredo residents. It specializes in cabrito, with Mexican dishes such as *mollejas* (sweetbreads) and *sesos* (brains) served with *borracho* beans. Watch the chefs smoke the cabrito in the glassed-in kitchen, then enjoy the diner atmosphere of this authentic Mexican restaurant. $.

west

day trip 01

west

gateway to mexico:
eagle pass; piedras negras, mexico

eagle pass

It's 142 miles southwest on US 57 from San Antonio to Eagle Pass and its sister city, Piedras Negras. These destinations are popular for a weekend of shopping, partying, and south-of-the-border fun.

The drive to Eagle Pass goes quickly, following I–35 south to US 57, which leads through miles of fertile farmland before it hits the mesquite-filled country near the border. You'll find basic services in Devine, but gas stations are few and far between from this farming community until you reach the border.

Eagle Pass, a city of more than 25,000 residents, was founded after the Texas Revolution when Mexico prohibited all trade with Texas. Smugglers began a new route to the north. The Texas militia set up an observation camp at a crossing called Paso del Aguila (Eagle Pass), named for the birds nesting in the area. Soon settlers began coming to the area. In 1849 the U.S. Infantry built Fort Duncan to defend the new territory from Indian attack. The fort later was used during the Civil War and manned by Confederate soldiers.

Like other border towns, Eagle Pass is bilingual. Many Mexican citizens cross the border to shop at the large Mall de las Aguilas and in the downtown dress and specialty shops. For Americans, much of Eagle Pass's appeal lies in its proximity to Mexico. Many visitors spend the cooler hours shopping in Piedras Negras, then return to Eagle Pass for a swim and an evening meal.

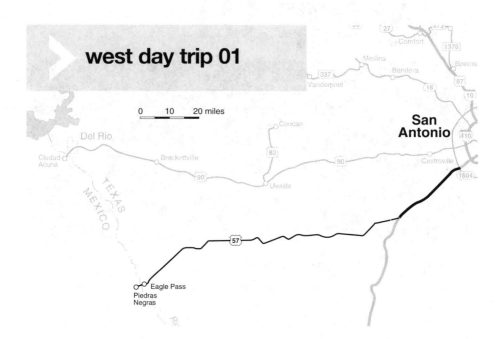

west day trip 01

0   10   20 miles

Del Rio

Cludad
Acuna

TEXAS
MEXICO

Brackettville

Concan

San
Antonio

Castroville

Uvalde

57

Eagle Pass
Piedras
Negras

where to go

Fort Duncan Park. (830) 773–4343. From Main Street (US 57), turn south on South Adams Street. Here you can take a self-guided tour of eleven original structures, including barracks and the headquarters building that's home to the Fort Duncan Museum. The museum presents displays on the early history of the old Indian fort and Confederate outpost. The fort saw its final action from 1890 to 1916, when National Guard units were attached to the command following disturbances in Mexico. Park is open daily; museum is open afternoons only. Free.

where to eat

Kettle Restaurant. 2525 Main Street (US 57) in front of La Quinta Inn; (830) 773–7263. This chain restaurant is open twenty-four hours a day for breakfast, lunch, and dinner. $$.

Charcoal Grill. Mall de las Aguilas, 455 South Bibb (off US 57); (830) 773–8023. This family-style restaurant specializes in charcoal-grilled steaks and burgers, all brought to your table with a bowl of sliced jalapeños. $$.

where to stay

La Quinta Motor Inn. 2525 Main Street (US 57); (800) 531–5900; www.lq.com. This comfortable family motel, offering a palm-shaded swimming pool, sits just five minutes from the border. $$.

piedras negras, mexico

From Eagle Pass, you can walk or drive across the International Bridge to Piedras Negras, named for the "black rock" (anthracite coal) found in the area after flooding on the Rio Grande. This city of more than 100,000 residents is a gateway to interior Mexico for many tourists, who follow Mexico Highway 57 to Saltillo.

Drivers must purchase short-term Mexican auto insurance before entering the country. (American insurance policies are generally not valid in Mexico, where automobile mishaps are a criminal rather than a civil offense.) Coverage is available from Capitol Insurance at 1115 Main Street in Eagle Pass (830–773–2341). (See Appendix A, "Entering Mexico," for more information.) Across the border, it's best to use secured parking, available for a small fee on the Plaza Principal, the main square, and at several restaurants and motels in town.

In Piedras Negras, as in other border towns, you may drink the water in the better hotels and restaurants. In other establishments, order bottled water or bring your own.

Piedras Negras's main square is filled with park benches, stately shade trees, and vendors selling food and drink. It's a nice place to sit for a while and watch the fascinating activity that is Old Mexico. From the main square, follow Zaragoza Street to the Mercado Municipal Zaragoza, the primary tourist market, about 3 blocks away. The walk takes you past Mexican music stores, several bars, *zapaterias* (shoe stores), and *roperias* (dress shops).

The Mexican peso was reevaluated in 1993, when three decimal places were dropped. Formerly you may have seen a $150,000 price tag on a dress. Today that price would be marked N$150 (150 *nuevo,* or new, pesos). Within the market, goods are marked in both dollars and pesos. The prices are open to *negociación,* a traditional way to purchase items in Mexico. T-shirts, Mexican dresses, serapes, blankets, chess sets, and men's Mexican wedding shirts are all very popular choices in the mercado. (See Appendix B, "Shopping in Mexico," for pointers.)

To dial a number in Piedras Negras from the United States, first dial the international code (011), then the country code (52), then the telephone number.

where to stay

La Quinta Motor Inn. Avenue East Carranza 1205; (878) 2–7479. This family motel, located a few miles from the market area, includes a restaurant and bar. All forty-two rooms are air-conditioned and include cable TV and telephones. $.

Holiday Inn Piedras Negras. Avenue Lazaro Cardenas (south Mexico Highway 57); (878) 3–0646; www.ichotelsgroup.com. This white motel is located about fifteen minutes from the market area. All rooms are air-conditioned and include a television and telephone. The motel also has a beautiful swimming pool and courtyard. $$.

day trip 02

west

multicultural miles:
castroville, hondo,
uvalde, concan

castroville

Castroville is only 20 miles west of San Antonio on US 90, but it's another world in terms of mood and atmosphere. This small town serves up a mixture of many cultures: French, German, English, Alsatian, and Spanish. It's best known for its Alsatian roots and sometimes is called the Little Alsace of Texas.

The community was founded by Frenchman Henri Castro, who contracted with the Republic of Texas to bring settlers from Europe. These pioneers came from the French province of Alsace in 1844, bringing with them the Alsatian language, a Germanic dialect. Today only the older residents of Castroville carry on this mother tongue.

Although the language has dropped out of everyday use, many Alsatian customs and traditions have survived. The city still sports European-style homes with nonsymmetrical, sloping roofs. The Alsatian Dancers of Texas perform folk dancing at many festivals, including the town's St. Louis Day celebration. (See "Festivals and Celebrations" at the back of this book.)

Castroville is usually busy on weekends, as San Antonio residents come to shop the town's numerous antiques stores, dine in the Alsatian restaurants, and tour the historical sites.

where to go

Landmark Inn State Historical Park. 402 East Florence Street; (830) 931–2133; www.tpwd.state.tx.us. The Texas Parks and Wildlife Department operates the historic Landmark Inn and museum. The inn was first a home and general store before becoming the Vance Hotel. Robert E. Lee and Bigfoot Wallace, a famous Texas Ranger, were said to have stayed here on the banks of the Medina River.

During World War II the hotel was renamed the Landmark Inn. Aside from accommodations (see "Where to Stay"), the inn contains displays illustrating Henri Castro's early efforts to recruit settlers as well as exhibits covering early Castroville life. Also recommended is a self-guided tour of the beautifully manicured inn grounds. Open daily. Free.

Castroville Walking Tour. (830) 538–3142; www.castroville.com. Pick up a free map from the chamber of commerce to see sixty-five points of interest, from Civil War–era homes to an 1845 church.

Castroville Regional Park. South off US 90; (830) 931–4070. Camp along the banks of the Medina River or enjoy swimming, picnicking, or walking in this park. Fee for camping hookups and picnic table use.

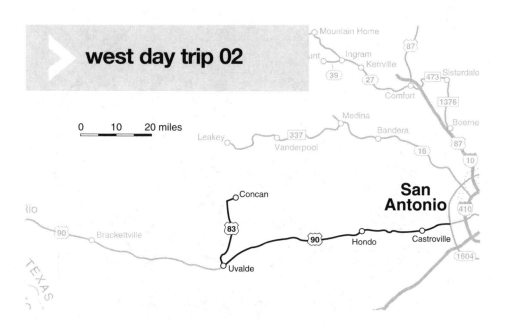

> # west day trip 02

where to eat

Alsatian Restaurant. 403 Angelo Street; (830) 931–3260. Housed in a historic nineteenth-century cottage typical of the provincial homes of Castroville, this restaurant specializes in Alsatian and German food, including spicy Alsatian sausage, crusty French bread, home-made noodles, and red sauerkraut. Steaks and seafood also are served. If it's a nice day, don't miss the chance to dine outside in the open-air *biergarten.* Open daily for lunch; dinner Thursday through Sunday. $$.

Haby's Alsatian Bakery. 207 US 290 East; (830) 931–2118. With Castroville's rich Alsatian and German heritage, you know the town has to have a great bakery. Well, here it is. You can choose from apple strudel, molasses cookies, and fresh-baked breads. Open Monday through Saturday. $.

where to stay

Landmark Inn State Historical Park. 402 Florence Street; (830) 931–2133 or (512) 389–8900 (for reservations). Guests at this historic inn can stay in one of eight beautifully

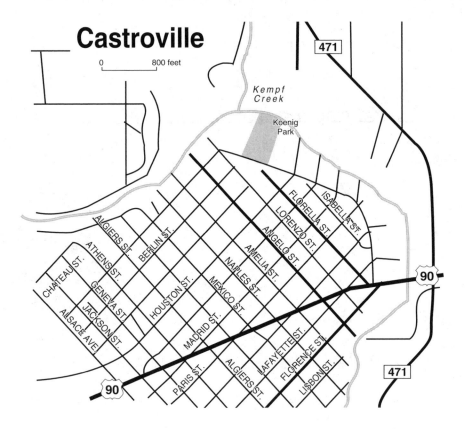

appointed rooms as well as in a separate cottage that may have once served as the only bathhouse between San Antonio and Eagle Pass. All rooms have air-conditioning; most rooms come with private baths; none have telephones or television. Make your reservations early, especially for weekends. $.

hondo

Continue west from Castroville on US 90 to the community of Hondo, once a railroad stop. Hondo (which means "deep" in Spanish) is a center for ranching and farming.

where to go

777 Exotic Game Ranch. (830) 426–3476. US 90 2 miles west of Hondo to Richter Lane; follow signs. The 777 might look vaguely familiar, even if you've never been to Hondo in the past, thanks to the movie *Ace Ventura: When Nature Calls*. This sprawling ranch, filled with exotic species from around the globe, was used as a set for the Jim Carrey movie; sets from the production can be seen on the property. The ranch is used for hunting, fishing, and photography of exotic species. Reservations required.

uvalde

Continue west on US 90 to Uvalde, located on the Leona River in the last outreaches of the Hill Country.

Spanish settlers came to this area in 1674. A century later they attempted to construct missions to convert the Lipan-Apache Indians, the foremost of the Apache groups in Texas. This plan was soon abandoned because of repeated Indian attacks on the mission. The Apaches were defeated in 1709 by Spanish military leader Juan del Uvalde in what's now known as Uvalde Canyon.

where to go

Garner Memorial Museum. 333 North Park Street; (830) 278–5018. This was once the home of Uvalde's most famous citizen: John Nance Garner, vice president of the United States during Franklin Roosevelt's first and second presidential terms. The museum is filled with reminders of Garner's political career. Open Monday through Saturday; extended hours during summer months. Fee.

Uvalde Grand Opera House. 100 West North Austin Street; (830) 278–4184. Even if a performance isn't scheduled, this 1891 opera house deserves a peek. Tours can be arranged on weekdays. Free.

Fort Inge County Park. One and a half miles south of Uvalde on FM 140. This park is located at the site of Fort Inge, a cavalry post that dates from 1849. Travelers find picnic sites as well as hiking trails and camping here, along with good bird-watching. The park is located on the Leona River. Open daily. Free.

Briscoe Art and Antique Collection. 200 East Nopal Street; (830) 278–6231. On display at the First State Bank, this multimillion-dollar art collection was developed by former Texas governor Dolph Briscoe and his wife. Pieces from artists ranging from Rembrandt to Salinas are on display. Tours are available. Open weekedays. Free.

National Fish Hatchery. FM 481, 1 mile south of Uvalde; (830) 278–2419. This hatchery specializes in endangered fish species, but visitors will also find good bird-watching here as well as hiking and picnicking. Open weekdays. Free.

where to shop

Market Square Antiques. 103 North West Street; (830) 278–1294. This downtown antiques dealer houses wares by many dealers. Look for antique furniture, collectibles, jewelry, and gift items. Open daily.

Opera House Antiques. 100 West North Street; (830) 278–9380. Housed on the first floor of the Uvalde Grand Opera House, this shop contains antiques and collectibles. Open Monday through Saturday.

Joe Pena Saddle Shop. 2521 East Main; (830) 278–6531. This longtime shop has produced leather items for actors Nick Nolte and John Wayne as well as the Texas Rangers. The shop is located inside Uvalco Supply. Call for hours.

South Texas Fine Woods. 4326 US 90E; (830) 278–1832. Hand-carved mesquite furniture is showcased in this retail shop. Tours of the workshop are also available. Open Monday through Saturday.

Coleman's Stained Glass. 710 East Main; (830) 278–8351. This shop sells stained glass in many forms; classes are also available. Open Tuesday through Saturday.

where to eat

Rexall Drug and Soda Fountain. 201 North Getty Street; (830) 278–2589. Step back to the days of old-time soda fountains at this favorite eatery. Sandwiches, burgers, and Blue Bell ice cream top the menu. Open Monday through Saturday for lunch. $.

Evett's Barbecue. 301 East Main; (830) 278–6204. This casual eatery serves traditional Texas barbecue fare—brisket, sausage, and chicken—on picnic tables. Open Tuesday through Saturday. $–$$.

Town House Restaurant. 2105 East Main Street; (830) 278–2428. The menu at this casual restaurant offers a taste of several Texas favorites: Tex-Mex, seafood, and, of course, chicken-fried steak. Open for breakfast, lunch, and dinner daily. $$.

where to stay

Holiday Inn. 920 East Main; (830) 278–4511. This 150-room hotel includes a restaurant, pool, and laundry facilities, and offers room service. $$.

concan

Word has it that this town is named for *coon can,* a Mexican gambling game. Today it's a safe gamble for outdoor recreation from swimming to camping.

where to go

Garner State Park. (830) 232–6132; www.tpwd.state.tx.us. Thirty-one miles north of Uvalde on US 83 or 8 miles north of Concan on the Frio River. From US 83, turn east on FM 1050 for a half mile to Park Road 29.

Named for John Nance Garner, this beautiful state park is located on the chilly, spring-fed waters of the Frio River (*frio* means "cold" in Spanish). There are campsites, screened shelters, cabins with double beds, an eighteen-hole miniature golf course, and a 1-mile hiking trail built by the Civilian Conservation Corps during the 1930s. The highlight of the park is the river, filled with swimmers, inner-tubers, and paddleboats during the warmer months.

Other activities include bike riding along a surfaced trail more than a half mile in length, hiking 5½ miles of trails, miniature golf in season, and paddleboating. Campers can bring their own facilities or rent a screened shelter or cabin. (The park is so popular that travelers who rent a cabin on either Friday or Saturday night must take both nights.) Open daily. Fee.

day trip 03

west

wild, wild west:
brackettville; del rio; ciudad acuña, mexico;
seminole canyon state historical park

This weekend trip has a lot to offer, from shoot-'em-up fun at Alamo Village to an afternoon dip in Del Rio's San Felipe Springs. Hop across the border for some bargain shopping, a margarita, and a Mexican dinner in Ciudad Acuña. The next day, take your choice of Del Rio's historic sites, a cruise on Lake Amistad, or a look at prehistoric drawings in Seminole Canyon.

brackettville

It's a quick 120 miles down US 90 from San Antonio to Brackettville. (For attractions along this highway, see West Day Trip 02.)

Brackettville is the home of Fort Clark, built by the U.S. Cavalry in 1852 to protect the frontier from hostile Indians. Several important soldiers were stationed here over the years, including Gen. George S. Patton. During World War II, Fort Clark served as a German POW camp. At the conclusion of that war, the fort was deactivated. Although Fort Clark's military days may be over, today the compound has taken on a new role as a resort, its stone barracks converted to modern motel rooms. There's also an RV park nearby.

where to go

Old Guardhouse Jail Cavalry Museum. US 90, in Fort Clark Springs; (830) 563–9150. Famous generals who served at Fort Clark are featured in this museum, along with the many troops who passed through the post. Open weekend afternoons. Free.

Alamo Village. (830) 563–2580. North of Brackettville; turn off US 90 on FM 674 and continue for 7 miles. This family amusement theme park, located on a 30-square-mile ranch, is often used as a movie set. It features a replica of the Alamo, built in the mid-1950s for the filming of *The Alamo* starring John Wayne. Since that time, many movies, commercials, documentaries, and TV shows have been shot here.

While there are no amusement rides, visitors can tour the John Wayne Museum, filled with pictures and posters from his many films, as well as an Old West jail (complete with cells), a blacksmith's shop, a chapel, and a bank that's been the scene of many movie holdups. During summer months, gunslingers bite the dust four times a day at showdowns staged in front of the cantina. Open daily except the Christmas holidays. Fee.

Kickapoo Cavern State Park. Twenty-two miles north of Brackettville on RR 674; (830) 563–2342; www.tpwd.state.tx.us. This undeveloped park is open only to travelers who make prior arrangements. The park contains fifteen known caverns, including Kickapoo Cavern. The caves are home to populations of Brazilian free-tailed bats during warm weather months. The park offers guided tours of the caves for those interested in spelunking; this is not a

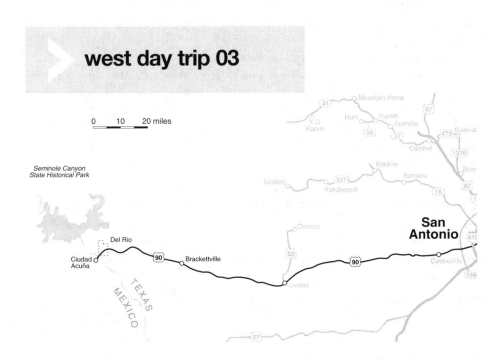

west day trip 03

typical cave tour with lighting and wide paths. At press time the park was closed for general visits, but it can be visited on scheduled group tours. For a schedule visit the park Web site. Fee.

where to stay

Fort Clark Springs Motel and RV Park. US 90, in Fort Clark Springs; (830) 563–9210. The stone barracks of this 1872 fort have been renovated into modern motel rooms. Guests have access to a pool, plus nine- and eighteen-hole golf courses. $$.

del rio

Located 32 miles west on US 90 from Brackettville, Del Rio is the most popular border town within reach of San Antonio. It's a year-round paradise for anglers, hunters, boaters, and archaeology buffs. Many Texas border towns serve primarily as overnight stops after a day in Mexico, but Del Rio is its own main attraction. Museums, historic sites, fishing, camping, bird-watching, and boating all await within thirty minutes of downtown.

Another feature that separates Del Rio from other border cities is its abundance of water. The town is literally an oasis in the semiarid climate at the edge of the Chihuahuan Desert. Tall palm trees, lush lawns, and a golf course dotted with water hazards are all part of Del Rio. The San Felipe Springs pump ninety million gallons of water daily. The crystal-clear water has drawn inhabitants to this region for 10,000 years, from prehistoric Indians who lived in the canyons west of here to Spanish missionaries who named the area San Felipe del Rio in 1635.

Today the San Felipe Springs provide water for the city of Del Rio, offering a cool swim on a hot summer day. At the San Felipe Amphitheater, the water is diverted through a stone moat separating the audience from a stage used for concerts and special events.

Del Rio lies 12 miles from the Amistad Dam and Lake Amistad, both the result of a cooperative effort between Mexico and the United States.

where to go

Val Verde Winery. 100 Qualia Drive; (830) 775–9714; www.valverdewinery.com. Italian immigrant Frank Qualia established this winery in 1883, drawn to the area by its flowing springs and fertile land. The oldest winery in Texas, this enterprise is now operated by third-generation vintner Thomas Qualia. Val Verde produces many wines, including award-winning Don Luis Tawny Port. Tours and tastings are available on a drop-in basis. Open daily except Sunday. Free.

Whitehead Memorial Museum. 1308 South Main Street; (830) 774–7568; www.white head-museum.com. This museum is best known for its replica of the Jersey Lilly, Judge Roy

> ## judge roy bean

Buried in Del Rio, Judge Roy Bean, the self-proclaimed "Law West of the Pecos," was undoubtedly one of the most colorful characters in the American West. From behind the bar of the Jersey Lilly, his saloon in the railroad town of Langtry, Judge Bean served up frontier justice along with beer and whiskey.

Perhaps the strangest story concerns his obsession with the British actress Lilly Langtry, who was popularly known as "The Jersey Lily." Bean named his saloon in her honor and wrote her numerous letters, begging her to visit her namesake town in Texas. So persistent were his entreaties that after several years (and his implication that the town was named for her), Lilly Langtry consented to make a stop there on a 1904 tour. In March 1903, a few months before she arrived, Bean died.

Bean's saloon and courtroom. (The original Jersey Lilly remains in Langtry, about 60 miles west of Del Rio.) Judge Bean and his son Sam are buried behind the replica of the saloon, their graves marked with simple headstones. The museum boasts more than twenty exhibit sites, including an 1870s store, a windmill, a log cabin, a caboose, and the Cadena Nativity, a cultural folk art exhibit. Open Tuesday through Saturday and Sunday afternoon. Fee.

Lake Amistad. West of Del Rio on US 90. The construction of Lake Amistad (derived from the Spanish word for friendship) was a cooperative project between the United States and Mexico. The 67,000-acre lake was completed in 1969 as a way to control flooding, provide irrigation for South Texas farms and ranches, and offer water recreation. Surrounded by 1,000 miles of shoreline, the reservoir contains thirty-five species of fish, including striper, bass, crappie, perch, catfish, gar, and sunfish. You must have separate fishing licenses for the U.S. and Mexican areas of the lake. Both Texas and Mexico fishing licenses are sold in the marinas and in many Del Rio stores.

The 6-mile-long Amistad Dam is responsible for the creation of the enormous lake. The observation deck affords a look at the 86-mile-long reservoir. Atop the dam stand two bronze eagles, each 7 feet tall, symbolizing the two participating countries and marking the international border.

Tlaloc, the Rain God. Mexican shore of Lake Amistad, near Amistad Dam. This 23-foot stone statue is a replica of one carved by the Teotihuacán people years before Aztec rule in Mexico. Tlaloc is believed to bring rain. Some swear the statue works, pointing to the higher-than-normal rainfalls in the years following the dam's construction.

Lake Amistad Resort and Marina. US 90, Diablo East Recreation Area; (830) 774–4157. Concessioners at the marina rent small powerboats and large houseboats sleeping up to ten people. You can cruise to the main part of Lake Amistad or up the Devil's River to some clear, spring-fed swimming holes. Open daily. Free admission; fee for rentals.

Lake Amistad Tours. The historic pictographs of the Lower Pecos are featured on this boat tour. Coast Guard–approved 30-foot boats are used, and tours are led by photographer Jim Zintgraff. His work is now the only record of many pictographs that were lost when Lake Amistad was formed. Fee. For reservations, call (830) 775–6484, or write HCR #3, Box 44, Del Rio, TX 78840.

where to eat

Wright's Steak House. US 90, 3 miles west of the intersection of US 277; (830) 775–2621. This casual steak house features all the usual cuts plus choices like Texas-size chicken-fried steak. Save room for home-baked cheesecake, then work off that big dinner on the dance floor. Closed Monday. Dinner only Tuesday through Saturday; lunch and dinner Sunday. $$.

Cripple Creek Saloon. US 90 West; (830) 775–0153. Modeled after the original Cripple Creek Saloon in Colorado, this restaurant specializes in prime rib but also serves up a mean sirloin, filet mignon, and rib eye. Seafood, from lobster to coho salmon to swordfish, rounds out the menu. Closed Sunday. $$–$$$.

where to stay

Del Rio offers a wide array of accommodations: mom-and-pop motels, popular chains, fishing resorts, and bed-and-breakfasts. For a complete listing call the Del Rio Chamber of Commerce at (800) 889–8149 or (830) 775–3551; write 1915 Veterans Boulevard, Del Rio, TX 78840; or visit www.drchamber.com.

Ramada Inn. 2101 Veterans Boulevard; (800) 272–6232 or (830) 775–1511; www.ramada inndelrio.com. This popular 155-room motel is conveniently located on the main thoroughfare through town, offering guests a pool, hot tub, workout room, restaurant, and bar. $$.

Villa del Rio. 123 Hudson Street; (800) 995–1887 or (830) 768–1100; www.villadelrio.com. This nineteenth-century mansion is tucked beneath stately palms and pecan trees. Guests can stroll to Texas's oldest winery or enjoy a leisurely day in one of four suites that feature fireplace foyers, hand-painted tiled floors, and an atmosphere that recalls the days of South Texas haciendas. $$.

especially for winter texans

Del Rio has a very active winter-visitor community. The chamber of commerce hosts a Winter Visitors Welcome Party, an arts and crafts fair, and an appreciation party during the season.

The Welcome Party is held on the first weekend in December and includes a traditional Texas meal. Exhibits introduce newcomers to local attractions, and gold cards offering discounts at area businesses are distributed. The Winter Artist Crafts Fair kicks off in February, giving participants a chance to sell arts and crafts without the usual booth expense associated with such shows. In mid-March, Del Rio throws its big Winter Visitors Festival.

The chamber publishes a calendar of special events planned for winter visitors, including dessert cook-offs, Mexican shopping trips, museum tours, and more. For a copy, call the Del Rio chamber at (800) 889–8149 or (830) 775–3551, or see www.drchamber.com.

ciudad acuña, mexico

To reach the international border and Ciudad Acuña, take Spur 239 off Highway 90. Most travelers drive to the Texas side of the International Bridge and pay a small fee for secured parking. From there you can take a cab or a bus (every thirty minutes) across the river or walk across the toll bridge.

A bus takes shoppers from Del Rio across the border to the Acuña (pronounced "a-COON-ya") shopping district. This place is filled with tourist shops, especially along Hidalgo Street. There is no central market here, but the shops are continuous for several blocks as you enter town.

To place telephone calls to Mexico, first dial the international code (011), then the country code (52), followed by the phone number.

where to shop

El Caballo Blanco (The White Horse). Hidalgo 110; no phone. This leather shop is filled floor to ceiling with handbags, billfolds, *huaraches,* boots, saddles, and even gun holsters. Look for traditional Mexican purses, hand-tooled with cactus, Aztec, and eagle designs. Open daily.

Nick's Warehouse. Hidalgo 185; (877) 2–6731. Nick's calls itself the largest handmade dress shop in Acuña, and it is. Beautifully embroidered items in festive colors fill the racks, from infant clothes to one-size-fits-all women's dresses. Open daily.

Casa Uxmal (Artesanías Mexicanas). Hidalgo 125; (877) 2–0925. This shop has a little of everything, from abalone inlay jewelry and Mexican dresses to hand-blown glass. Open daily.

where to eat

Crosbys. Hidalgo 195; (877) 2–2020. Both Americans and Mexicans frequent this lively restaurant for a good meal and a good time. From the etched glass and oak doors to the white columns separating the dining rooms, the look says "elegant," but the atmosphere definitely shouts "party." The menu features Tex-Mex food, steaks, seafood, and *de la presa la Amistad*—fish from nearby Lake Amistad. Try the *Camarón Relleno Estilo Crosbys* (shrimp stuffed with cheese and wrapped in bacon) or share a sampler platter, a massive tray of breaded quail, frog's legs, stuffed shrimp, and beef strips. The margaritas are king-size and served in glasses resembling goldfish bowls.

Service on Friday and Saturday nights can be slow by American standards. Open daily for lunch and dinner. $$.

seminole canyon state historical park

To reach the entrance of Seminole Canyon State Historical Park, drive west about 45 miles on US 90 from Del Rio, 9 miles past the town of Comstock. This is a stop archaeology buffs shouldn't miss. During the warmer months, make this an early morning trip because the canyon can be very hot during the afternoon.

Seminole Canyon was occupied by early humans about 8,500 years ago. Little is known of that early culture, but archaeologists believe these people were hunter-gatherers, living on plants and small animals. The former residents left paintings on the caves and canyon walls that represent animals, Indians, and supernatural shamans, but their meaning is still unknown. Sadly, these artifacts are fading, and it is unknown how much longer the images will last. Scientists currently are studying ways to slow the deterioration.

Visitors can see the pictographs on a ninety-minute guided tour conducted Wednesday through Sunday at 10:00 A.M. and 3:00 P.M. This is a somewhat strenuous 1-mile hike, so bring along a small canteen of water (there are no drinking facilities in the canyon). The trip also takes in Fate Bell Shelter, named for the archaeologist who discovered the pictographs.

In the park campground, both tent and trailer sites are available, along with electrical and water hookups. Open daily. Fee. For more information on camping, call (915) 292–4464; write Park Superintendent, Seminole Canyon State Historical Park, P.O. Box 820, Comstock, TX 78837; or see www.tpwd.state.tx.us.

northwest

day trip 01

northwest

cowboy country:
bandera, medina, vanderpool

bandera

Follow TX 16 northwest for 50 miles to Bandera, "the Cowboy Capital of the World." This town is well known for its plentiful dude ranches, country-western music, rodeos, and horse racing.

Once part of the "Wild West," Bandera Pass, located 12 miles north of town on TX 173, was the site of many battles between Spanish conquistadors and both Apache and Comanche Indians. Legend has it that following a battle with the Apaches in 1732, a flag (or *bandera* in Spanish) was hung at the pass to mark the boundary between the two opposing forces.

Bandera has open rodeos weekly from Memorial Day to Labor Day. Typically rodeos are held Tuesday night at Mansfield Park and Saturday night at Twin Elm Guest Ranch. For more schedule information call the Bandera Convention and Visitors Bureau at (800) 364–3833 or see www.banderacowboycapital.com.

Today the wildest action in town occurs in the dance halls every night except Monday and Tuesday. Put on your boots, crease your best jeans, and get ready to two-step with locals and vacationers alike.

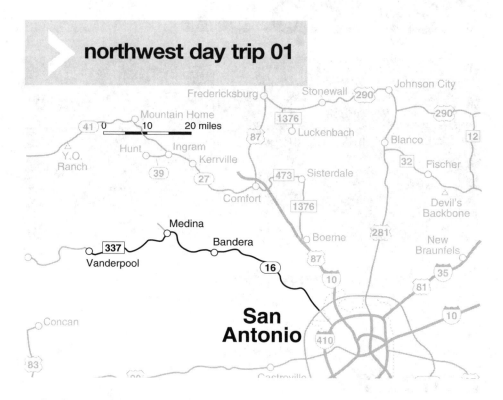

northwest day trip 01

where to go

Frontier Times Museum. Thirteenth Street, 1 block north of the courthouse; (830) 796–3864; www.frontiertimesmuseum.com. Established in 1927, this museum is a good place to learn more about Bandera's early days. The stone building is filled with cowboy paraphernalia, Indian arrowheads, and prehistoric artifacts. Its most unusual exhibit is a shrunken head from Ecuador, part of a private collection donated to the museum. Open daily. Fee.

Historical Walking Tours. Have a look at the buildings that witnessed Bandera's evolution from a frontier town to a vacation destination with a self-guided tour. Thirty-two sites along the route lead visitors to the county courthouse, the Old Jail, Bandera's first theater, and many homes that date from the community's earliest days. Pick up your walking tour brochure at the Bandera County Visitors Center, 1808 TX 16 South (800–364–3833). Free.

Hill Country State Natural Area. (830) 796–4413; www.tpwd.state.tx.us. South on TX 173 to FM 1077, then right for 12 miles. This rugged park preserves 5,400 acres of Hill Country land. Only primitive camping is available; you must bring your own water and pick up and remove your own trash. This park was originally open primarily for equestrian use, but today it has become popular with hikers and bicyclists. There are 34 miles of quiet trails and camp areas for backpackers and equestrians. Cool off with a dip in West Verde Creek or fish for catfish, perch, or largemouth bass. Horse rentals are available off-site. Open Thursday through Monday. Fee.

Medina River. TX 16, east of town. The cypress-lined Medina River is a popular spot during the summer months, when swimmers, canoeists, and inner-tubers enjoy the cool water. The Medina can be hazardous during high water, however, with rocky rapids and submerged trees. There is public access to the river from the TX 16 bridge in town.

Running-R Ranch Trail Rides. Eleven miles from Bandera off FM 1077; (830) 796–3984; www.rrranch.com. Enjoy one-, two-, or three-hour rides with an experienced wrangler. The ranch also offers all-day rides with a picnic and cowboy cookout. Children six and up are accepted. Fee.

The Silver Dollar Bar. 308 Main Street; (830) 796–8826. Pick up a longneck, grab a partner, and start boot-scootin' at this Texas honky-tonk. Owner and singer Arkey Blue performs country-western hits here as crowds fill the sawdust-covered dance floor.

where to shop

Love's Antiques Mall. 310 Main Street; (830) 796–3838. Located in the historic Carmichael and Hay store, this antiques mall features custom-crafted western furniture, wrought iron, sculpture, and collectibles.

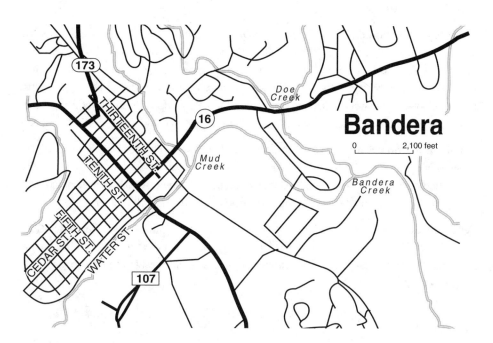

where to stay

The country around Bandera is dotted with dude ranches. Rates usually include three meals daily as well as family-style entertainment and supervised children's programs. Horseback riding is often part of the weeklong package. A minimum stay of two or three days is required at most ranches during peak summer season.

For a complete listing of Bandera's dude ranches, as well as other accommodations and campgrounds, call the Bandera Convention and Visitors Bureau at (800) 364–3833.

Mayan Ranch. TX 16, 2 miles west of Bandera; (830) 796–3312; www.mayanranch.com. For more than forty years this sixty-room ranch has entertained vacationers with cowboy breakfasts, cookouts, horseback riding, fishing, and hayrides. Summer also brings organized children's programs. Rooms are appointed with western-style furniture. Call for rates.

Dixie Dude Ranch. (800) 375–YALL; www.dixieduderanch.com. South on TX 173 1½ miles to FM 1077, then southwest for 9 more miles. Five generations of the Whitley family have welcomed guests to this nineteen-room ranch since 1937.

The Dixie Dude Ranch offers potential cowpokes the opportunity to enjoy a taste of ranch life. Start your morning with a leisurely trail ride for a genuine cowboy breakfast, then enjoy a day filled with hiking, hunting for Indian arrowheads, country and western dance lessons, fishing, and horseshoes. You can even participate in a rodeo twice a week. The ranch includes nineteen units made up of individual cottages, duplex cabins, and lodge rooms featuring early Texas architecture. Rates include meals and two horseback rides daily. Call for rates.

Flying L Guest Ranch. (800) 292–5134; www.flyingL.com. From TX 16, turn south on TX 173 for 1½ miles, then left on Wharton Dock Road. This 542-acre ranch has thirty-eight guest houses, each with two rooms, a refrigerator, a microwave, a coffee pot, and a TV. You can choose many different packages offering horseback riding, hayrides, and even golf at the ranch's eighteen-hole course. During the summer there's a supervised children's program, plus nightly entertainment ranging from western shows to "branding" parties. Call for rates.

Silver Spur Dude Ranch. Ten miles south of Bandera on FM 1077; (830) 796–3037; www.ssranch.com. Pull on your boots and grab your Stetson before heading to this 275-acre ranch near the Hill Country State Natural Area. You'll stay busy out of the saddle with fishing, tubing, canoeing, and golf, plus swimming in the ranch pool. Call for rates.

Twin Elm Guest Ranch. A half mile off FM 470 from TX 16 (4 miles from Bandera); (888) 567–3049 or (830) 796–3628; www.twinelmranch.com. This 200-acre dude ranch is on the Medina River. All the usual cowboy activities are available, from fishing to horseback riding and horseshoe pitching. Call for rates.

LH7 Ranch Resort. FM 3240 (5 miles from Bandera); (830) 796–4314. This 1,200-acre ranch, which raises longhorn cattle, has cottages with kitchenettes plus RV hookups. There's plenty to keep any cowpoke busy, including fishing in a fifty-acre lake, hayrides, horseback riding, and nature walks. Call for rates.

Bandera Lodge. 700 TX 16 South; (830) 796–3093. This forty-four-room lodge offers trail rides as well as a restaurant and bar, a pool, and cable TV. $.

taking a shine to medina

If there's any truth to the saying "an apple a day keeps the doctor away," then the physicians of Medina, Texas, better close up shop. This Hill Country community is the capital of Texas's apple industry, a business that's growing by the bushel.

Medina's apple industry took root in 1981 when Baxter Adams and his wife, Carol, moved to Love Creek Ranch outside Medina. Baxter spent thirty years as an exploration geologist before moving to this region, a land of rocky, rugged hills, with fertile valleys irrigated by Love Creek, a cool, spring-fed creek that originates on the ranch.

These valleys gave Adams the idea for an orchard, one that wouldn't take a lot of land. "I don't have much tillable land," Adams explained. "I've got to really make it count. It's a matter of trying to squeeze the most possible dollars out of the smallest possible area."

And that's just what Baxter Adams has done.

This Texas version of Johnny Appleseed specializes in dwarf apple trees, which reach a height of only 5 or 6 feet. The Lilliputians boast full-size apples, however, up to fifty pounds per tree, in varieties from Red Delicious to Gala and Crispin.

Baxter and Carol started with 1,000 trees in 1981, and they were soon in the apple business. Unlike the full-size trees that take seven years to produce a crop, the dwarfs yield fruit in just a year and a half. Another advantage Adams has over the northern producers is his growing season: Texas apples ripen weeks before their northern cousins.

Every July, the Hill Country celebrates this blooming industry with the International Apple Festival. The party begins with a street dance and continues with family activities, including contests for best apple, best apple pie, and best apple anything. There is also a quilt contest, volleyball championship, and, for the energetic, a "triapple-on."

especially for winter texans

Besides the dude ranches, Bandera has excellent RV parks. Many weekly activities are of special interest to the Winter Texans who call Bandera home. Country-western dances are held Wednesday through Saturday, and there's bingo on Friday. For a complete listing call the Bandera Convention and Visitors Bureau at (800) 364–3833.

medina

From Bandera, continue west on TX 16 to the tiny community of Medina, best known for its dwarf apple trees that produce full-size fruit in varieties from Crispin to Jonagold.

where to go

Love Creek Orchards. RR 337, west of Medina; (800) 449–0882 or (830) 589–2588; www.lovecreekorchards.com. From May through October these beautiful orchards are open to the public by guided tour only; call to set up a tour time. Free.

where to shop

The Cider Mill and Country Store. Main Street (TX 16), downtown; (830) 589–2202. This shop offers Love Creek apples for sale from June through November. Butter, sauces, vinegars, jellies, syrups, pies, breads, and even apple ice cream are sold here year-round. If you're ready to start your own orchard but you're short on room, you can buy "the patio apple orchard," a dwarf tree grown on a trellis in a wooden planter. Open daily.

vanderpool

Vanderpool is a quiet getaway during all but the fall months. Tucked into the hills surrounding the Sabinal River, this small town is a center for sheep and goat ranching.

where to go

Lost Maples State Natural Area. (830) 966–3413. West on RR 337 to the intersection of RR 187; turn north and continue for 5 miles. This state park is one of the most heavily visited sites in Texas during October and November, when the bigtooth maples provide some of the best color in the state. Weekend visits at this time can be very crowded, so note that the parking here is limited to 250 cars. The best time to visit is during midweek, when you can enjoy a walk into the park without crowds. For information on fall colors, call (800) 792–1112 or check out the Web site www.tpwd.state.tx.us.

There are 10 miles of hiking trails to enjoy all year along the Sabinal River Canyon. In the summer, visitors can swim and fish in the river. Camping includes primitive areas on the

leaf peeping

Are you starting to dream about the feel of a cool autumn breeze? To hear the crackle of leaves beneath your feet? To smell the smoke of an evening campfire?

Central and South Texas may not have the blazing colors of New England, but you will find a brilliant quilt of fall colors if you look.

The top destination for many leaf peepers is Lost Maples State Natural Area in Vanderpool. The maples, located so far from other specimens of the beautiful tree, may seem lost, but there's no doubt that the park itself has been found: It's one of the most heavily visited sites in Texas in the fall.

Fall colors generated by blazing sumacs, sycamores, chinaberries, and cottonwoods can be seen along the scenic drive along RR 1050 from Utopia to US 83. RR 337 from Camp Wood to Leakey is another favorite of ours, as is the Devil's Backbone Scenic Drive, a stretch of RR 32 from Wimberley to Blanco.

To find out the status of fall colors, call the Texas Travel Information Center at (800) 452–9292 or the Texas Parks and Wildlife hot line at (800) 792–1112. The brilliant colors require cold night temperatures, an occurrence that can reach the Hill Country valleys long before the warmer city locations.

hiking trails and a thirty-site campground with restrooms and showers as well as a trailer dump station. Open daily. Fee.

Scenic Drive. Utopia to US 83. West of Utopia, RR 1050 winds its way through the Hill Country, crossing the Frio River before eventually intersecting with US 83 north of Concan. During late fall, the drive is dotted with blazing sumacs, sycamores, chinaberries, and cottonwoods. Free.

Scenic Drive. RR 337. This drive from Camp Wood to Leakey (pronounced "LA-key") is often termed the most scenic in Texas and is an excellent spot for fall color. The road climbs to some of the highest elevations in the Hill Country at more than 2,300 feet, and roadside lookouts offer great vistas of reds, greens, and golds. Free.

day trip 02

northwest

western art:
leon springs, kerrville, ingram,
hunt, y. o. ranch

Head northwest of San Antonio on I–10, and you'll soon see the city fall away and surrender the road to the Hill Country. Not far beyond the loops that lasso San Antonio into a
metropolitan corral lies a land of white-tailed deer and oak-dotted hills, a gateway to the Hill
Country for I–10 travelers.

leon springs

Leon Springs is a popular stop for folks driving west and for city residents looking for a few
hours of country living with a little antiques shopping, a plate of good food, and a chance to
two-step their cares away. But Leon Springs's role as a travelers' stop is not a new one.
Before the days of speeding cars, Leon Springs was a stagecoach stop offering travelers
services of all kinds. A German immigrant named Max Aue built a stagecoach stop and later
added a storefront and supplies area. When he married, Aue constructed a log cabin
nearby. The businessman saw another opportunity, though, and word has it that the entre-
preneur later added a brothel upstairs above his home!

where to eat

Rudy's. I–10W and Boerne Stage Road; (210) 698–2141; www.rudys.com. A former grocery store is now the home of the Leon Springs Cafe. The son of Max Aue, Rudolph Aue
ran a grocery store and gas station at this site in 1929. Today the old Rudolph's Garage is

Rudy's Country Store and Bar-B-Q, another success story for restaurateur Phil Romano, founder of Romano's Macaroni Grill. Rudy's claims to be the home of the "Worst Bar-B-Que in Texas." Rudy's barbecue, cooked in German-style pits where the meat is never in direct contact with the heat or flames, is served with Rudy's famous sauce. The concoction of Doc Holliday's mother, once a general manager of the restaurant, the sauce is now shipped worldwide. $$.

where to go

Leon Springs Dancehall. I–10W; (210) 698–7070; www.leonspringsdancehall.com. The Leon Springs Dancehall opened in 1993, and since that time thousands of boots have scooted across the 18,000-square-foot dance hall and 10,000-square-foot backyard. Housed beneath a giant tin roof, the dance hall specializes in country and western music with free lessons every Wednesday through Friday. From Wednesday through Saturday the dance hall shakes a leg with up to 1,500 people two-steppin' their way around the dance floor, pitching horseshoes or washers, or playing volleyball. A 50-foot bar serves as a popular watering hole.

northwest day trip 02

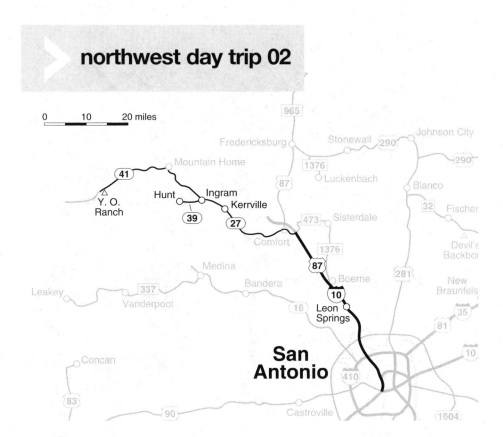

kerrville

From Leon Springs, continue west on I–10 through Boerne and Comfort before exiting at TX 27 for the final 19 miles. For attractions in Boerne and Comfort, be sure to read Northwest Day Trip 03.

Kerrville is popular with retirees, hunters, Winter Texans, and campers. The town of more than 20,000 residents is home to a 500-acre state park and many privately owned camps catering to youth and church groups. Started in the 1840s, the town was named for James Kerr, a supporter of Texas independence who died in the Civil War. With its unpolluted environment and low humidity, Kerrville later became known as a health center, attracting tuberculosis patients from around the country. The town is still considered one of the most healthful places to live in the nation because of its clean air and moderate climate.

Throughout Kerrville the Schreiner name appears on everything from Schreiner College to Schreiner's Department Store. Charles Schreiner, who became a Texas Ranger at the tender age of fifteen, came to Kerrville as a young man in the 1850s. Following the Civil War, he began a dry goods store and started acquiring land and raising sheep and goats. The Charles Schreiner Company soon expanded to include banking, ranching, and marketing

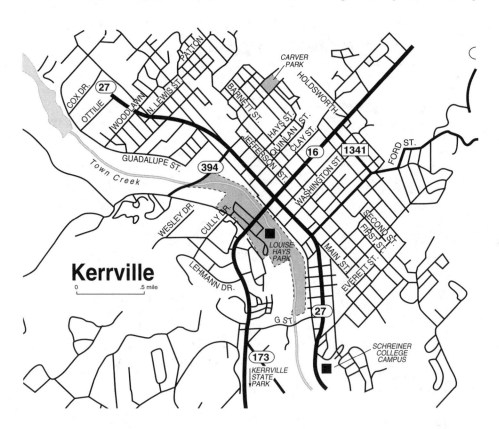

art walk

Many Hill Country communities offer monthly markets featuring arts and crafts, but Kerrville takes their special event one step further. The Second Saturday Art Trail offers visitors not only the chance to shop for art but to visit the city's growing number of galleries. From 10:00 A.M. to 6:00 P.M. on the second Saturday of every month, the city's galleries (now more than two dozen strong) open their doors, provide special demonstrations, serve refreshments, and help introduce all the members of the family to various types of artwork. For more see www.artinthe hills.com.

wool and mohair. This was the first business in America to recognize the value of mohair, the product of Angora goats. Before long, Schreiner made Kerrville the mohair capital of the world.

In 1880 Schreiner acquired the Y. O. Ranch, which grew over the next twenty years to more than 600,000 acres, covering a distance of 80 miles. Today the Schreiner family still owns this well-known ranch, located in nearby Mountain Home.

where to go

Museum of Western Art. 1550 Bandera Highway (TX 173); (830) 896–2553; www.museum ofwesternart.org. This hilltop museum (formerly the Cowboy Artists of America Museum) features work by members of the Cowboy Artists of America. The building is constructed of eighteen boveda brick domes, an old construction method used in Mexico. Western-themed paintings and sculpture fill the museum. Visitors also can take in special programs on the folklore, music, and history of the Old West. Open Tuesday to Saturday and Sunday afternoons. Fee.

Hill Country Museum. 226 Earl Garrett Street; (830) 896–8633. This local-history museum traces the development of Kerrville. Housed in Charles Schreiner's former mansion built in 1879, the museum has granite porch columns, wooden parquet floors, and a bronze fountain imported from France. Open Monday through Saturday. Fee.

Kerrville-Schreiner State Park. 2385 Bandera Highway, 1 mile southwest on TX 173; (830) 257–5392; www.tpwd.state.tx.us. This park offers 7 miles of hiking trails, as well as fishing and swimming in the Guadalupe River. During summer months, inner tubes and canoes are for rent for an afternoon excursion on the river. Mountain bikers will find 6 miles of beginner/intermediate trails. Campsites include water, electricity, sewage hookups, and screened shelters. Fee.

Louise Hays City Park. Off TX 16 at Thompson Drive; (830) 792–8386. Bring your picnic lunch to this beautiful spot on the Guadalupe River. Paddleboats are available for rent, and ducks and cypress trees abound. Days only. Free.

where to shop

James Avery, Craftsman. Three and a half miles north of Kerrville on Harper Road; (830) 895–1122. Since 1954 James Avery has been one of Texas's premier silversmiths. He began crafting silver crosses and religious symbols, but today his work includes gold and silver renditions of many subjects, from prickly pears to dolphins. Retail shop open Monday through Saturday, visitor center open weekdays.

Artisan Accents. 826 Water Street; (830) 896–4220. Both regional and nationally recognized artists are showcased at this gallery. Housed in a building that served as a bakery a century ago, the gallery features decorative arts, wearable art, furnishings, and fine art. Open weekdays.

Sunrise Antique Mall. 820 Water Street; (830) 257–5044. Kerrville's largest antiques shop is housed in a century-old building that once served as a furniture store. Today the mall features everything from antique furniture to other antiques and artwork. Open Monday through Saturday.

where to eat

Bill's Barbecue. 1909 Junction Highway; (830) 895–5733. This barbecue eatery serves up Texas favorites such as brisket, sausage, and chicken with the obligatory side dishes. Open Tuesday through Saturday for lunch. $$. No credit cards.

Joe's Jefferson Street Cafe. 1001 Jefferson Street; (830) 257–2929. This elegant eatery, housed in a Victorian mansion, serves up Texas and Southern favorites such as shrimp, catfish, and steak. Open for lunch weekdays, dinner Monday through Saturday. $$–$$$.

Kathy's on the River. 417 Water Street; (830) 257–7811. This restaurant is an excellent spot for those looking for outdoor dining with a view of the river. The menu offers a little bit of everything, from traditional chicken-fried steak to dishes with an Asian flair. $$–$$$. Open Tuesday through Sunday.

where to stay

Y. O. Ranch Resort Hotel and Conference Center. 2033 Sidney Baker, at TX 16 and I-10; (830) 257–4440; www.yoresort.com. This 200-room hotel salutes the famous Y. O. Ranch in Mountain Home, located 30 miles from Kerrville. The lobby is filled with reminders of the area's major industries—cattle and hunting. Twelve hotel suites include amenities such as fireplaces, furniture covered in longhorn hide, and wet bars. In keeping with the Wild

West spirit, the hotel has a bar called the Elm Water Hole Saloon and a swim-up bar dubbed the Jersey Lilly. $$.

especially for winter texans

Kerrville is home to more than a dozen RV parks, some of which are designated adults only. For a listing contact the Kerrville Convention and Visitors Center at (800) 221–7958 or see www.kerrrvilletexascvb.com. The Kerrville Chamber of Commerce (830–896–1155) can provide a listing of condominium and apartment properties with short-term leases. A welcoming committee greets Winter Texans as well as the many retirees who relocate to the area.

ingram

To reach Ingram, leave Kerrville on TX 27 and continue northwest for 7 miles. This small community on the banks of the Guadalupe River was started in 1879 by the Reverend J. C. W. Ingram, who built a general store and post office in what is now called Old Ingram.

Old Ingram, located off TX 27 on Old Ingram Loop, is home to many art galleries and antiques shops. Ingram proper lies along TX 27. It features stores and outfitters catering to white-tailed deer, turkey, and quail hunters. The town is particularly busy during deer season, from November to early January. Hunting licenses are required and are sold at local sporting-goods stores. For more information call the Texas Parks and Wildlife Department at (800) 792–1112 in Texas or (512) 389–4800 elsewhere, or write 4200 Smith School Road, Austin, TX 78744.

where to go

Kerr County Historical Murals. At TX 27 and TX 39. Sixteen murals decorate the T. J. Moore Lumber Company building, the work of local artist Jack Feagan. The scenes portray historical events in Kerr County, starting with the establishment of shingle camps (where wooden roofing shingles were produced in 1846). Other paintings highlight cattle drives, the birth of the mohair industry, and the last Indian raid.

Hill Country Arts Foundation. TX 39, west of the Ingram Loop; (800) 459–HCAF or (830) 367–5121; www.hcaf.com. The foundation, located 6 miles west of Kerrville in Ingram, is one of the oldest multidiscipline arts centers in the nation. For more than three decades, this fifteen-acre center on the banks of the Guadalupe River has encouraged students in the fields of art, theater, photography, printmaking, and even quilt making. American musicals and plays are performed during the summer months at the open-air Point Theatre; indoor shows entertain audiences at other times throughout the year. A gallery exhibits the work of many artists and is open daily. The Gazebo Gift Shop is a sales outlet for local artists, open Monday through Friday afternoons. Call for a schedule of play times or special events.

where to shop

Guadalupe Forge. TX 27, just off TX 39; (830) 367–4433; www.guadalupeforge.com. You can have your own brand made in this blacksmith shop. Its walls are decorated with cattle brands ranging from simple initials to more elaborate renderings of stars or the rising sun. Open Monday through Saturday.

Southwestern Elegance. Old Ingram Loop; (830) 367–4749. This unique store specializes in Mexican collectibles and antiques (especially primitives), Mennonite furniture, and Tarahumara Indian collectibles. Open daily; call for hours.

hunt

Continue west on TX 39 for 7 miles to Hunt, a small community best known for its year-round outdoor recreational camps catering to Scouts as well as youth and church groups.

where to go

Kerr Wildlife Management Area. RR 1340, 12 miles northwest of Hunt; (830) 238–4483. Enjoy a driving tour over this 6,493-acre research ranch owned by the Texas Fish and Game Commission. Purchased to study the relationship between wildlife and livestock, the ranch is home to white-tailed deer, javelinas, wild turkeys, bobcats, gray foxes, and ringtails. Pick up a booklet at the entrance or write Kerr Wildlife Management Area, Route 1, Box 180, Hunt, TX 78024. Open daily, but call during hunting season, when the area may be closed for a hunt. Free.

Stonehenge II. FM 1340, just out of Hunt; no phone. Located on private land, this replica of England's Stonehenge may be viewed from a roadside parking area. A sign provides information on the original Stonehenge and its smaller Texas cousin. Open daily. Free.

y. o. ranch

From Hunt, head west on FM 1340 to TX 41. Turn left, and the Y. O. Ranch will soon appear on your right. This ranch dates from 1880, a part of the 550,000 acres purchased by Capt. Charles Schreiner, former Texas Ranger and longhorn cattle owner.

Presently the Y. O. spans 60 square miles and supports more than 1,000 registered longhorns, the largest such herd in the nation. Charlie Schreiner III, the original owner's grandson, brought the breed back from near extinction in the late 1950s, founding the Texas Longhorn Breeders Association. The Y. O. hosts a longhorn trail drive at the ranch each spring.

After a devastating Texas drought in the 1950s, the Schreiners began to diversify their ranch, stocking the land with the largest collection of natural roaming exotics in the country, including many rare and endangered species. More than 10,000 animals range the hills, including zebra, ostrich, giraffe, emu, and ibex.

You may visit the Y. O. Ranch by reservation only. Both day and overnight programs are offered. Day-trippers can enjoy the spread on a lunch tour or photo safari. The ranch also hosts an Outdoor Awareness Program, an environmental education camp that teaches horseback riding, rappelling, gun handling, and wildlife study. Overnight accommodations are available in the 1880s-era cabins; meals are included. For general information call (800) YO–RANCH or (830) 967–2624.

day trip 03

northwest

german heritage:
boerne, comfort, sisterdale

This is an easy day trip from San Antonio, a journey through three small towns that share a strong German heritage. Although the excursion begins on sleek I–10, it includes some curving farm-to-market (FM) roads that are very susceptible to flooding. If it's raining heavily, save this trip for another day!

boerne

To reach Boerne (pronounced "Bernie"), take I–10 northwest for 22 miles to a spot filled with history, antiques, and natural attractions. Boerne is located on the banks of Cibolo Creek in the rolling Texas Hill Country. The community was founded in 1847 by German immigrants, members of the same group who settled nearby New Braunfels. They named the town for author Ludwig Börne, whose writings inspired many people to leave Germany for the New World.

During the 1880s, Boerne became known as a health spot, and vacationers came by railroad to soak in mineral water spas and enjoy the clean country air. Although no mineral spas remain today, Boerne still offers a quiet country atmosphere and dozens of antiques shops.

Boerne is also home to the Boerne Village Band. For more than a century this German band (the oldest continuously active German band in the country and the oldest in the world outside of Munich) has entertained residents and visitors with its old-world sound. This group can be heard at many local festivals and at Boerne's own Abendkonzerte, summer concerts scheduled for selected Tuesday nights throughout the summer on the Main Plaza.

where to go

Chamber of Commerce. 1 Main Plaza, beside Ye Kendall Inn; (888) 842–8080. Stop here for brochures and maps to Boerne attractions and shopping areas. Open daily Monday through Friday and Saturday morning.

Agricultural Heritage Center. TX 46, 1 mile from Main Street; (830) 249–6007. This museum features farm and ranch tools used by pioneers in the late nineteenth and early twentieth centuries, including a working steam-operated blacksmith shop. Six acres surrounding the museum are covered with hand-drawn plows, wagons, early tractors, and woodworking tools. Open Sunday and Wednesday afternoons. Free.

Cascade Caverns. (830) 755–8080; www.cascadecaverns.com. From I–10 take exit 543 and follow signs on Cascade Caverns Road; This family-owned cavern, located in a 105-acre park, has a 100-foot waterfall, an unusual underground sight. Guided tours take forty-five minutes. Open daily. Fee.

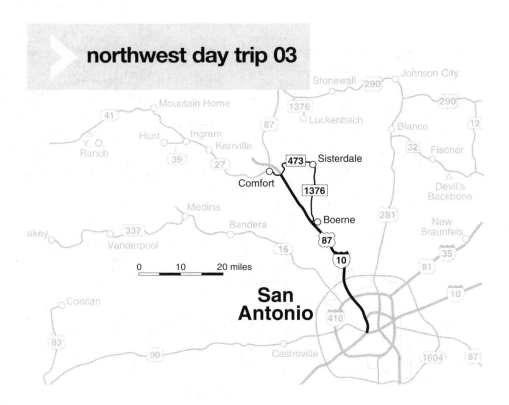

northwest day trip 03

Cave Without a Name. 325 Kreutzberg Road; (830) 537–4212; www.cavewithoutaname .com. Guided tours take groups through six rooms of this family-owned cavern. A subterranean river and numerous cave formations fill the tour. Open daily. Fee.

Cibolo Wilderness Trail. Boerne City Park, TX 46 at Cibolo Creek; (830) 249–4616. Enjoy grassland, marshland, and woodland in this park that offers a slice of the Hill Country. The wilderness area includes both reclaimed prairie and reclaimed marsh, with walking trails that range from ¼ mile to 1 mile in length. Free.

Kuhlmann-King Historical House and Graham Building and Museum Store. Main Street and Blanco Road; (830) 249–2030. The Kuhlmann-King House was built by a local businessman for his German bride in 1885. Today the two-story stone home is staffed by volunteer docents. The Graham Building, located next door, is home to the Boerne Area Historical Preservation Society and exhibits on local history. Open Saturday and Sunday afternoons. Free.

Guadalupe River State Park. Thirteen miles east of Boerne off TX 46 on Park Road 31; (830) 438–2656. The star of this park is the clear, cold Guadalupe River. Camp, swim, hike, or just picnic on its scenic banks. On Saturday mornings, take an interpretive tour of the Honey Creek State Natural Area to learn more about the plants and animals of the region. Fee.

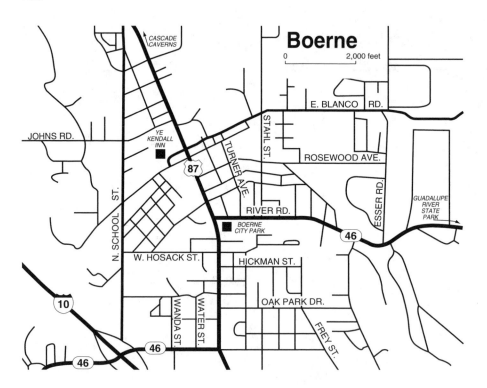

Honey Creek State Natural Area. Spring Branch, 13 miles east of Boerne off TX 46 on Park Road 31; (830) 438–2656. Use of this park is limited to those on guided tours. A two-hour guided look at the park's history and ecology is offered every Saturday morning at 9:00 A.M.; reservations aren't necessary, but call first to confirm that a tour will be offered. Access into the park is through the Guadalupe River State Park. Fee.

where to eat

Limestone Grill. 128 West Blanco Street, Main Plaza; (830) 249–2138. In 1859 the owners of this two-story structure began renting rooms to stagecoach travelers, eventually developing the property into an inn. Over the years, its famous guests have included Confederate president Jefferson Davis and U.S. president Dwight D. Eisenhower. Along with seven bed-and-breakfast rooms furnished with period antiques, the inn includes a restaurant with adjoining bar that serves favorites such as burgers, salads, and soups along with specialties like lemon chicken schnitzel, chicken-fried steak, and Gulf shrimp. Open daily for lunch; dinner Tuesday through Saturday. $$.

Peach Tree Kountry Kitchen. 448 South Main Street; (830) 249–8583. This casual eatery serves up good, old-fashioned family fare such as meat loaf and chicken-fried steak. Open for lunch Tuesday to Saturday. $$.

where to stay

Ye Kendall Inn. 128 West Blanco Street; (800) 364–2138. This historic inn still offers thirteen antiques-filled guest rooms. Amenities at the property include a restaurant (see "Where to Eat"), a bar, and easy access to downtown shops. $$–$$$.

comfort

From Boerne, continue north on I–10 for 17 miles to road marker 524 and exit to the town of Comfort. This small community is big in history and attractions. The downtown area is a National Historic District, filled with homes and businesses built by early settlers.

Comfort was founded in 1854 by German pioneers who wanted to name the town Gemütlichkeit, meaning peace, serenity, comfort, and happiness. After some deliberation, though, they decided on the easier to pronounce Comfort instead.

Today Comfort offers tourists numerous historic buildings to explore, filled with antiques shops and restaurants. Visitors will also find a historic inn and the oldest general store in Texas. Weekends are the busiest time to visit, but even then the atmosphere is relaxing, unhurried, and, well, comfortable.

where to go

Treue der Union (True to the Union) Monument. High Street, between Third and Fourth Streets; (830) 995–3131. During the Civil War, German residents of Comfort who did not approve of slavery and openly swore their loyalty to the Union were burned out of their farms. The Confederates responsible also lynched locals who refused to pledge their allegiance to the movement. Several German farmers decided to defect to Mexico but were caught by Confederate soldiers and killed on the banks of the Nueces River, their bodies left unburied.

Finally retrieved in 1865, the remains were returned to Comfort and buried in a mass grave. A white obelisk, the oldest monument in Texas and the only monument to the Union located south of the Mason-Dixon Line, was dedicated here in 1866. One of only six such sites in the country, the shrine recently received congressional approval to continually fly the flag at half-mast. The flag that waves here has thirty-six stars, the same number it had when the marker was dedicated in 1866. Free.

Bat Roost. FM 473, on private land; (830) 995–3131. As you leave Comfort for Sisterdale, this historic structure sits 1 mile from town on the right side of the road behind private gates. While it's generally known now that bats feed on disease-spreading mosquitoes, the folks here have known about the importance of these furry mammals since 1918, when Albert Steves constructed hygieostatic bat roosts in an experimental attempt to control malaria. The roosts were intended to encourage the area's large bat population to remain in the region. Only sixteen such roosts were built in the country, and this is the oldest of three known still to exist. Free, but just view from the road.

Bat Tunnel. Fifteen miles northeast of Comfort off TX 473 on old Highway 9; (830) 995–3131. View the evening flight of 1.2 million Mexican free-tailed bats from this abandoned railroad tunnel now managed by the Texas Parks and Wildlife Department. Closed October to May. Free.

where to shop

The Comfort Common. 818 High Street; (830) 995–3030. This combination bed-and-breakfast inn and indoor shopping area is located within the historic Ingenhuett-Faust Hotel. Several buildings behind the hotel display antique primitives and furniture. Open daily.

Bygone Days. High Street; (830) 995–3003. This year-round Christmas store features handmade Santa Claus figures as well as numerous antiques, all in a historic building with original counters and fixtures. Open daily.

where to eat

Cypress Creek Cafe. 408 West TX 27; (830) 995–3977. Order up Texas fare such as chicken-fried steak, T-bones, or lighter dishes such as seafood and sandwiches at this casual restaurant. Open daily. $–$$.

where to stay

The Comfort Common. 818 High Street; (830) 995–3030. A bed-and-breakfast operating within the 1880 Ingenhuett-Faust Hotel, The Comfort Common's five suites are decorated in English country, American country, and Victorian decor. All rooms include private baths and period furnishings. The backyard cottage has a fireplace and complete kitchen. All rates include breakfast. As rooms book quickly for weekends, consider a midweek stay. $$.

sisterdale

From Comfort, head out on FM 473 to nearby Sisterdale, best known as the home of a small winery. The burg, like nearby Boerne, was settled by a group of intellectuals. Today the population has dwindled to a handful of residents, and you have to look carefully to keep from passing right through town.

where to go

Sister Creek Vineyards. FM 1376, off FM 473; (830) 324–6704; www.sistercreekvineyards.com. These vineyards thrive in "downtown" Sisterdale, located between the East and West Sister Creeks. The winery, a restored cotton gin, produces traditional French wines. Open daily for self-guided tours. Free. For more information write to Route 2, P.O. Box 2481 C-1, Sisterdale, TX 78806.

Sisterdale General Store. FM 473; (830) 324–6767. This historic general store and adjoining bar have served generations of customers. The bar sells Sister Creek Wine. Closed Monday.

regional information

north

day trip 01

Blanco Chamber of Commerce
312 Pecan
P.O. Box 626
Blanco, TX 78606
(830) 833–5101
www.blancochamber.com

Wimberley Chamber of Commerce
14100 RR 12 North
P.O. Box 12
Wimberley, TX 78676
(512) 847–2201
www.wimberley.org

day trip 02

Johnson City Chamber of Commerce
P.O. Box 485
Johnson City, TX 78636
(830) 868–7684
www.johnsoncity-texas.com

Stonewall Chamber of Commerce
P.O. Box 1
Stonewall, TX 78671
(830) 644–2735
www.stonewalltexas.com

Fredericksburg Convention and Visitors Bureau
302 East Austin
Fredericksburg, TX 78624
(888) 997–3600 or (830) 997–6523
www.fredericksburg-texas.com

northeast

day trip 01

New Braunfels Chamber of Commerce
390 South Seguin Street
New Braunfels, TX 78130
P.O. Box 311417, New Braunfels, TX 78131
(800) 572–2626 or (830) 625–2385
www.nbjumpin.com

Gruene Information Center
1601 Hunter Road
New Braunfels, TX 78130
(830) 629–5077
www.gruene.net

day trip 02

San Marcos Chamber of Commerce
P.O. Box 2310
San Marcos, TX 78667
(888) 200–5620 or (512) 396–5900
www.sanmarcostexas.com

Buda City Hall
P.O. Box 1218
Buda, TX 78610
(512) 295–6331

day trip 03

Austin Convention and Visitors Bureau
301 Congress Avenue, Suite 200
Austin, TX 78701
(866) GO–AUSTIN or (512) 474–5171
www.austintexas.org

east

day trip 01

Luling Area Chamber of Commerce
P.O. Box 710
421 East Davis Street
Luling, TX 78648
(830) 875–3214
www.lulingcc.org

Flatonia Chamber of Commerce
P.O. Box 610
208 East North Main
Flatonia, TX 78941
(512) 865–3920
www.flatonia-tx.com

Schulenburg Chamber of Commerce
618 North Main
Schulenburg, TX 78956
(866) 504–5294 or (409) 743–4514
www.schulenburgchamber.org

day trip 02

Seguin Convention and Visitors Bureau
427 North Austin Street
Seguin, TX 78155
P.O. Box 710, Seguin, TX 78156
(800) 580–7322 or (830) 379–6382
www.visitseguin.com

Gonzales Chamber of Commerce
P.O. Box 134
Gonzales, TX 78629
(830) 672–6532
www.gonzalestexas.com

Shiner Chamber of Commerce
P.O. Box 221
810 North Avenue E
Shiner, TX 77984
(361) 594–4180
www.shinertx.com

Yoakum Chamber of Commerce
P.O. Box 591
Yoakum, TX 77995
(512) 293–2309
www.yoakumareachamber.com

day trip 03

Lockhart Chamber of Commerce
P.O. Box 840
205 South Main Street
Lockhart, TX 78644
(512) 398–2818
www.lockhart-tx.org

Bastrop Chamber of Commerce
927 Main Street
Bastrop, TX 78602
(512) 303–0558
www.bastropchamber.com

Smithville Area Chamber of Commerce
P.O. Box 716
100 First Street
Smithville, TX 78957
(512) 237–2313
www.smithvilletx.org

La Grange Chamber of Commerce
171 South Main Street
La Grange, TX 78945
(800) LAGRANGE or (979) 968–5756
www.lagrangetx.org

southeast

day trip 01

Goliad Chamber of Commerce
P.O. Box 606
Goliad, TX 77963
(800) 848–8674 or (361) 645–3563
www.goliadcc.org

day trip 02

Victoria Convention and Visitors Bureau
P.O. Box 2465
700 South Main, Suite 100
Victoria, TX 77902
(800) 926–5774 or (361) 573–5277
www.victoriachamber.org

Port Lavaca–Calhoun County Chamber of Commerce
Box 528
Port Lavaca, TX 77979
(800) 556–7678 or (361) 552–2959
www.portlavacainfo.com

south

day trip 01

Aransas Pass Chamber of Commerce and Visitors Center
130 West Goodnight
Aransas Pass, TX 78336
(800) 633–3028 or (361) 758–2750
www.aransaspass.org

Port Aransas Tourist and Convention Bureau
421 West Cotter
Port Aransas, TX 78373
(800) 45–COAST or (361) 749–5919
www.portaransas.org

Rockport-Fulton Area Chamber of Commerce
404 Broadway
Rockport, TX 78382
(800) 242–0071 or (800) 826–6441
www.rockport-fulton.org

day trip 02

Three Rivers Area Chamber of Commerce
P.O. Box 1648
Three Rivers, TX 78071
(888) 600–3115 or (361) 786–4330
www.threeriverstx.org

Greater Corpus Christi Convention and Visitors Bureau
1201 North Shoreline
Corpus Christi, TX 78403
(800) 678–OCEAN, (800) 766–2322, or (361) 881–1888
www.corpuschristi-tx-cvb.org

King Ranch Visitor Center
P.O. Box 1090
Kingsville, TX 78364
(361) 592–8055
www.king-ranch.com

Kingsville Convention and Visitors Bureau
1501 US 77
Kingsville, TX 78363
(800) 333–5032 or (361) 592–8516
www.kingsvilletexas.com

southwest

day trip 01

Dilley Chamber of Commerce
800 North Main
Dilley, TX 78017
(830) 334–9414
www.dilleychamber.org

Cotulla–LaSalle County Chamber of Commerce
290 North I–35
Cotulla, TX 78014
(800) 256–2326 or (830) 879–2326

Laredo Convention and Visitors Bureau
501 San Agustin
Laredo, TX 78040
(800) 361–3360 or (956) 795–2200
www.visitlaredo.com

west

day trip 01

Eagle Pass Chamber of Commerce
400 Garrison Street
Eagle Pass, TX 78853
(888) 355–3224 or (830) 773–3224
www.eaglepasstexas.com

day trip 02

Castroville Area Chamber of Commerce
P.O. Box 572
820 London Street
Castroville, TX 78009
(800) 778–6775 or (830) 538–3142
www.castroville.com

Hondo Area Chamber of Commerce
1607 Avenue K
Hondo, TX 78861
(830) 426–3037
www.rtis.com/reg/hondo

Uvalde Chamber of Commerce
300 East Main Street
Uvalde, TX 78801
(830) 278–3361
www.uvalde.org

day trip 03

Del Rio Area Chamber of Commerce
1915 Veterans Boulevard
Del Rio, TX 78840
(800) 889–8149 or (830) 775–3551
www.drchamber.com

northwest

day trip 01

Bandera County Convention and Visitors Bureau
P.O. Box 171
Bandera, TX 78003
(800) 364–3833 or (830) 796–3045
www.banderacowboycapital.com

day trip 02

Kerrville Convention and Visitors Bureau
1700 Sidney Baker, Suite 100
Kerrville, TX 78028
(800) 221–7958 or (830) 792–3535
www.kerrvilletx.com

West Kerr County Chamber of Commerce
P.O. Box 1006
Ingram, TX 78025
(830) 367–4322
www.wkcc.com

day trip 03

Greater Boerne Area Chamber of Commerce
126 Rosewood Avenue
Boerne, TX 78006
(888) 842–8080 or (830) 249–8000
www.boerne.org

Comfort Chamber of Commerce
P.O. Box 777
Seventh and High Streets
Comfort, TX 78013
(830) 995–3131
www.comfort-texas.com

festivals and celebrations

Texas undoubtedly has more festivals than any other state. Regardless of the weekend, you'll find some town whooping it up with parades, music, and lots of food. There are festivals for every interest, whether yours is pioneer heritage, German food, or watermelons.

For a quarterly list of Texas's annual events, write the Texas Department of Transportation at P.O. Box 5064, Austin, TX 78763-5064 or call (800) 8888–TEX or (512) 452–9292.

You can also view a free annual events calendar from the Texas Festivals and Events association at www.tourtexas.com/aroundtexas.html. You'll also find an online calendar on the *Texas Highways* magazine site, www.texashighways.com.

february

Celebration of Whooping Cranes, Port Aransas; (800) 45–COAST; www.portaransas .org/cranes.asp. This festival includes seminars, workshops, and tours dedicated to the endangered whooping cranes that winter at the Aransas National Wildlife Refuge. The special event, which includes birding tours, boat trips, and crafts shows, is scheduled for late February.

George Washington's Birthday Celebration, Laredo and Nuevo Laredo; (956) 722–0589. Since 1898 the border towns of Laredo and Nuevo Laredo have celebrated this holiday. Festivities run from Tuesday through Saturday with a *charro* rodeo, games, and a general party atmosphere.

Land of Leather Days, Yoakum; (512) 293–2309; www.yoakumtx.com. During the last weekend in February the importance of leather in "the Leather Capital of the World" is celebrated. There are saddle-making demonstrations, plus a chili cook-off and plenty of leather products for sale.

PRCA Rodeo, Victoria; (800) 926–5774. This annual event includes all the features of a traditional Texas rodeo, from riding to roping, along with western entertainment. Held at the Victoria Community Center.

Wine Lovers Trail, Fredericksburg; (830) 868–2321 or (830) 997–6523. More than a dozen Hill Country wineries participate in this event. Sample the products and enjoy special events.

march

Fulton Oysterfest, Fulton; (800) 242–0071 or (361) 729–2388. Spend the first weekend in March downing fried or raw oysters to celebrate the culmination of the oyster harvest. Besides oyster eating and shucking contests, there are games, entertainment, and dances.

Goliad County Fair and Rodeo, Goliad; (800) 848–8674 or (361) 645–2492. Cowboys and cowgirls compete in this rodeo that features precision riding, live entertainment, and more.

Goliad Massacre Reenactment. (361) 645–3563. This annual event re-creates Colonel Fannin and the Texas revolutionaries occupying the region and their battle with the Mexican army.

International Friendship Festival, Eagle Pass; (888) 355–3224. This event, with celebrations on both sides of the international border, includes a parade, carnival, and plenty of children's fun. Held in Shelby Park.

Star of Texas Fair and Rodeo, Austin; (512) 919–3000. Held at the Travis County Exposition and Heritage Center east of the city, this two-week event features nightly rodeos, live entertainment, and a livestock show.

SXSW (South by Southwest), Austin; (800) 888–8AUS. This event, held in mid-March, attracts more than 3,500 people from the music industry to the capital city for music conferences and nighttime entertainment. During the four-day festival, more than 400 acts perform at clubs throughout town. Wristbands permit music lovers to take in show after show, from rock to blues to Cajun music.

april

Artfest, Corpus Christi; (361) 883–0639. This event draws participating artists from around the state to show their artwork and to demonstrate the techniques used in its creation.

Buccaneer Days, Corpus Christi; (800) 678–OCEAN. Near the end of April, Corpus Christi's swashbuckling days are relived with pioneer parades, a terrific fireworks display over the bay, and a huge carnival.

Easter Fires, Fredericksburg; (830) 997–6523. Relive the Easter fires of 1847, when Comanches sat in the hills over Fredericksburg while women and children awaited the results of a peace talk. Mothers calmed their children's fears by explaining that the campfires belonged to the Easter Bunny. This story is re-created in a pageant on the Saturday eve before Easter. Advance tickets are suggested. For more information write Fredericksburg Easter Fires, P.O. Box 506, Fredericksburg, TX 78624.

Eeyore's Birthday Party, Austin; (800) 926–2282. Held the last Saturday of April, this is one of Austin's wackiest festivals, paying tribute to Eeyore of *Winnie-the-Pooh* fame. Outrageous costumes, live entertainment, food, drink, and games. A unique celebration of springtime.

Highland Lakes Bluebonnet Trail, Burnet, Buchanan Dam, Llano, and area communities; (512) 793–2803. The fragrant bluebonnet is the state flower of Texas. For two weekends in early April, a self-guided driving tour will take you past the area's prettiest bluebonnet fields. Each town on the trail, from Burnet to Llano, celebrates with art shows and a festival atmosphere.

Kerrville Easter Festival and Chili Classic, Kerrville; (800) 221–7958. Held at Schreiner College, this event features a cook-off, live music, an armadillo race, and an egg hunt.

River Rendezvous, La Grange; (800) 524–7264. This event draws canoeists from around the state. Visitors paddle down the Colorado River and enjoy camping, canoeing, fun, food, and old-fashioned storytelling.

Round Top Antiques Fair, Round Top; (281) 493–5501. Held the first weekend of April, this show features dealers from across the nation. It has been called the best antiques show in the state.

Smithville Jamboree, Smithville; (512) 237–2313. This longtime event includes parades, a livestock show, softball, volleyball and horseshoe tournaments, nightly dances, an antique car show, a carnival, and canoe races.

Texas Cactus Festival, Kingsville; (800) 333–5032. This annual event showcases the cacti of Texas through food, arts and crafts, and more. Live entertainment, as well as food tastings using cactus as an ingredient.

Texas Ladies' State Chili Cookoff, Seguin; (800) 580–7322. Women from around the state test their skills at this chili cook-off. Along with taste testings, visitors enjoy live entertainment.

Yesterfest and Salinas Art Festival, Bastrop; (512) 303–0558. Return to pioneer days on the banks of the Colorado River and try your hand at quilting, corn shucking, candle dipping, and doll making.

may

Chisholm Trail Roundup, Lockhart; (512) 398–2818. Relive the Battle of Plum Creek, where the Texas militia joined forces with Tonkowa Indians to defeat a band of Comanches. You can also enjoy a dance, a parade, and a carnival.

Cinco de Mayo and State Menudo Cook-off, San Marcos; (888) 200–5620. This festival is held on the weekend closest to Cinco de Mayo (May Fifth), the celebration of the Mexican victory over the French. Besides a carnival and musical performances, there's plenty of Mexican food, including *menudo* (a dish made from tripe, hominy, and spices).

Cinco de Mayo, Del Rio; (800) 889–8149 or (830) 775–3551. This border city celebrates its "Best of the Border" binational heritage at historic Brown Plaza.

Fiesta Laguna Gloria, Austin; (800) 926–2282 or (512) 474–5171. This festival combines art with the spirit of a Mexican party, complete with mariachis and Mexican folk dancers. More than 200 artists and crafters bring their work to this mid-May celebration.

Folkfest, New Braunfels; (830) 629–1572. This event, held at the Conservation Plaza and Texas Museum of Handmade Furniture, showcases the work of New Braunfels craftspeople and furniture makers through demonstrations, food, and live entertainment. Guided tours of local historic buildings are also available.

Funteer Days, Bandera; (800) 364–3833. If they had festivals back in the Wild West days, they must have looked like this one. Professional Rodeo Cowboys Association (PRCA) rodeo, arts and crafts, country-and-western dances, fiddlin' contests, and an Old West parade draw crowds for this weekend late in May.

Kerrville Folk Festival, Kerrville; (800) 221–7958 or (830) 257–3600; www.kerrville -music.com. This is one of the biggest outdoor music festivals in the state. For eighteen days Quiet Valley Ranch is filled with music lovers who come to hear both local and nationally known performers.

Pow Wow Festival, Laredo; (800) 795–2185. This annual event, held at the Laredo Civic Center grounds, showcases Native American food, dances, music, arts and crafts, and more.

Texas State Arts and Crafts Fair, Kerrville; (830) 896–5711; www.tacef.org. Every Memorial Day weekend, this festival opens its gates on the grounds of Schreiner College. Founded by the state of Texas, this enormous show features the paintings, sculptures, jewelry, and other artwork of more than 200 Texas artists, all available to answer questions about their work. A special children's area includes crafts instruction. Musical entertainment rounds out the day.

june

Boerne Berges Fest, Boerne; (888) 842–8080. This festival, scheduled for Father's Day weekend, includes arts and crafts, live music, and a celebration of summer.

Peach JAMboree, Stonewall; (830) 644–2735. The peach capital of Texas shows off its crop on the third Friday and Saturday of June. The local peach-pit–spitting record is more than 28 feet.

Watermelon Thump, Luling; (830) 875–3214. On the last Thursday, Friday, and Saturday of June, you can enjoy seed-spitting contests, watermelon-eating contests, and champion melon judging. There's also an arts and crafts show, carnivals, live entertainment, and street dances. A Guinness world record was set here in 1989 for spitting a watermelon seed almost 69 feet.

july

Deep Sea Roundup, Port Aransas; (800) 45–COAST; www.paboatmen.org. Anglers come from everywhere for a chance at the purse in the biggest fishing tournament on this part of the coast, held the weekend after July Fourth. Stay at the pier and watch the competitors weigh in their catch.

Fourth of July Celebration, Round Top; (979) 249–4042. One of the oldest celebrations of Independence Day winds through Round Top. For more information write the Round Top Chamber of Commerce, Round Top, TX 78954.

Frontier Days, Round Rock; (800) 747–3479. Come to Round Rock on the Friday and Saturday after the Fourth of July to watch a reenactment of the infamous shoot-out between outlaw Sam Bass and the Texas Rangers. There's also plenty of food, games, and the atmosphere of a summer festival.

Half Moon Holidays, Shiner; (361) 594–4180; www.shinertx.com. On the first Sunday in July, Shiner celebrates summer with a brisket cook-off, barbecue dinner, fireworks, a carnival, a horseshoe-pitching tournament, dancing, and lots of music.

International Apple Festival, Medina; (830) 589–2588. This celebration of the apple harvest is held in late July, with lots of apple pies, barbecue, and games.

July Fourth Parade, Seguin; (800) 580–7322. In July get ready for a red, white, and blue party known as the biggest small-town Fourth of July parade in Texas. The annual Freedom Fiesta has been drawing onlookers and participants since the early 1900s. The activities start with a patriotic parade, followed by food booths, arts and crafts, family entertainment, and kiddie rides for an old-fashioned street-fair atmosphere. In the evening, a street dance from 8:00 P.M. to midnight will keep the mood festive, as will the grand fireworks display in Max Starcke Park starting at 9:00 P.M.

Night in Old Fredericksburg, Fredericksburg; (830) 997–6523. This annual event, held on Market Square, showcases a different local culture every night through arts and crafts, food, dances, and more.

august

Gillespie County Fair, Fredericksburg; (830) 997–6523. This event holds the record as the longest running county fair in the state. The festivities include old-fashioned family fun, from carnival rides to food booths.

Grape Stomping Harvest Celebration, Tow; (512) 476–4477. Jump in a bin of red grapes and start stomping during this late August festival. Other activities include a cork toss, grape walk, hayrides, and music.

St. Louis Day, Castroville; (210) 538–3142. Since 1889, this Alsatian town has celebrated the feast day of St. Louis with a feast of its own on the Sunday closest to August 25. Local residents pitch in to prepare barbecue, Alsatian sausage, cabbage slaw, and potato salad, all served picnic-style in Koenig Park. The afternoon is filled with a country auction, arts and crafts, singers, and performances by the Alsatian Dancers of Texas.

september

Annual Republic of Texas Chilympiad, San Marcos; (800) 782–7653, ext. 177. Belly up to a bowl of red at this cook-off featuring more than 600 competitors. Arts and crafts, sporting events, a battle of the bands, and games are also featured.

Bayfest, Corpus Christi; (800) 242–0071. Along the bayfront, the city of Corpus Christi celebrates fall with boat races, fireworks, and a parade.

Comal County Fair, New Braunfels; (800) 572–2626. This long-running fair ranks as one of the largest (and one of the oldest) in the state. The event includes everything from a rodeo to carnival rides to children's play areas.

Deis y Seis de Septiembre, Del Rio; (800) 889–8149 or (830) 775–3551. First named San Felipe, Del Rio celebrates its historic past with Mexican food, Mexican bingo, and plenty of music.

Expomex, Nuevo Laredo; (800) 361–3360. This international festival celebrates with live music, dances, a carnival, and arts and crafts. Held at Carranza Park.

Fiesta en la Playa, Rockport; (800) 242–0071. This Labor Day weekend celebration with a south-of-the-border flair includes everything from tamale- and jalapeño-eating contests to a piñata contest to performances by Ballet Folklorico.

Hummer/Bird Celebration, Rockport; (800) 242–0071 or (361) 826–6441. Thousands of migrating hummingbirds stop to refuel in Rockport, which celebrates the event with four days of lectures by birding authorities, arts and crafts displays, boat tours, and Audubon-guided bus tours to sites swarming with hummingbirds.

Kerrville Wine and Music Festival, Kerrville; (830) 257–3600. The Hill Country town celebrates fall with performances by Texas musicians and tasting of Texas wines. Held at Quiet Valley Ranch, the site of the June Music Festival.

Port A Days, Port Aransas; (800) 45–COAST. This three-day farewell-to-summer festival starts with an "anything that will float but a boat" parade and includes a gumbo cook-off, a street dance, a horseshoe tournament, and lots of fine Gulf food.

october

Cajunfest, Bastrop; (512) 303–0558. This fall festival celebrates the Lone Star State's neighbors in Louisiana with Cajun food and drink, music, and even a live auction.

Come and Take It Days, Gonzales; (830) 672–6532. This reenactment of the famous "Come and Take It" skirmish that started the Texas Revolution takes place the first weekend in October. More than 30,000 visitors come to enjoy the battle as well as the games, a carnival, a *biergarten,* helicopter rides, and a street dance.

Czhilispiel, Flatonia; (512) 865–3920. When tiny Flatonia needed a doctor years ago, local citizens decided to send a hometown girl to medical school. To fund her education, they began this chili cook-off (now the second largest in Texas) and festival held in late October. There's lots of music, a quilt show, "the World's Largest Tented *Biergarten,"* and a barbecue cook-off as well.

Fiesta de Amistad, Del Rio and Ciudad Acuña; (800) 889–8149 or (830) 775–3551. The friendship between Del Rio and Ciudad Acuña is celebrated with a chili cook-off, a battle of the bands, and an international parade—the only one that starts in one country and ends in another.

Halloween on Sixth Street, Austin; (800) 888–8AUS. In the capital city, October 31 is not just for kids. The treat is the sight of thousands of revelers in wild costumes parading through the Sixth Street entertainment district. After the late-night bacchanalian outing, the trick may be getting up the next morning.

Missions Tour de Goliad, Goliad; (800) 848–8674. Bicyclists from around the state compete in this race. Riders select from four races ranging from 10 to 100 miles in length.

Oktoberfest, Fredericksburg; (830) 997–6523. On the first weekend in October, you can head to the "old country" by driving to this German Hill Country town. You'll find polka dancing and sausage galore, as well as arts and crafts, a street dance, and rides for the kids. Friday through Sunday.

Rockport Seafair, Rockport; (800) 242–0071. For more than two decades this coastal village has celebrated Columbus Day weekend with food and festivities. Crab races, a sailing regatta, and a gumbo cook-off keep the weekend busy.

Round Top Antiques Fair, Round Top; (281) 493–5501. Called by some the best such show in the state, this extravaganza features antiques dealers from across the United States. Held the first weekend of the month, it attracts shoppers from around the country.

november

Fall Arts Trail, Buchanan Dam, Kingsland, Burnet, Llano, and Marble Falls; (512) 756–4297. The Highland Lakes Arts Council sponsors this early November arts and crafts trail along the same route as the spring bluebonnet festival. Each community has an art show, including Buchanan Dam's Arts and Crafts Gallery, the oldest artists' cooperative in the United States.

Fredericksburg Food and Wine Fest, Fredericksburg; (830) 997–6523. In late October the Fredericksburg Food and Wine Fest highlights the top wineries of Texas. Along with award-winning vineyards, the event showcases more than forty vendors who offer a taste of Texas through spices, salsas, cheeses, and more. Two stages offer plenty of musical entertainment, and the whole family finds plenty of just-for-fun activities such as grape stomping and cork tossing.

Glowfest, New Braunfels; (800) 572–2626. Hot-air balloons illuminate the night with their kaleidoscope of colors like giant Christmas ornaments in the night sky. This event calls itself Texas's only winter holiday balloon festival and includes daytime balloon races. Balloons launch from Comal County Fairgrounds and the nightly "glow" takes place at Prince Solms Park.

Gospel Brunch, Gruene; (800) 572–2626. Holiday visitors won't want to miss Gospel Brunch with a Texas Twist, a special event that takes place in Gruene Hall. Put your hands together and enjoy the sounds of gospel in this New Orleans–inspired event that includes brunch and, for extra charge, plenty of libations. The brunch is held the second Sunday of November and December. The event runs from 10:45 A.M. to 1:00 P.M., and seating is very limited.

Mesquite Art Festival, Fredericksburg; (830) 997–6523. Visitors have the opportunity to shop for one-of-a-kind woodwork at this annual show, a gathering of more than fifty artists who work primarily in mesquite. The festival showcases collectibles, cabinets, mantels, sculptures, musical instruments, and other artwork made from the often maligned tree.

Old Gruene Market Days, Gruene; (830) 629–5077. Shoppers flock to this community during Old Gruene Market Days. The event includes plenty of arts and crafts, a farmers' market, and lots of live entertainment from 10:00 A.M. to 6:00 P.M. More than 125 vendors give you the chance to make holiday purchases along the streets in twenty-five shops and at the arts and crafts tent. Look for one-of-a-kind quilts, pottery, wreaths, jewelry, and other special items. During the Christmas Market Days, visitors will find plenty of activity celebrating the season. Enjoy live music at Gruene Hall on Saturday from 1:00 to 5:00 P.M. and on Sunday starting at noon; admission is free.

Wurstfest, New Braunfels; (800) 221–4369 or (210) 625–9167; www.wurstfest.com. Early in November, pull on your *lederhosen,* take out your beer stein, and join the fun at this celebration of sausage making. One of the largest German festivals in the country, Wurstfest features oompah bands and great German food.

december

Christmas in Goliad, Goliad; (800) 848–8674. This celebration gives the Christmas season a unique South Texas flavor that includes Pony Express stamp cancellation for cards, local arts and crafts, and a Las Posadas procession.

Christmas Lighting Tour, Johnson City, Llano, Fredericksburg, Blanco, Burnet, and Marble Falls. The Hill Country joins together for this trail of Christmas lights and festivities. Blanco's historic courthouse square is lit with festive lights, and Marble Falls celebrates with a walkway of lights every evening. Fredericksburg puts on a Kinderfest, Kristkindl Market, and candlelight tours of homes. Llano features a Santa Land. Johnson City, the boyhood home of LBJ, is aglow with more than a quarter million lights.

Harbor Lights, Corpus Christi; (800) 678–OCEAN. The Christmas spirit starts in Corpus Christi with the Christmas Tree Forest at the Art Museum of South Texas, with all trees decorated on a special theme. Santa Claus arrives in this port city aboard (what else?) a boat, and the bayfront twinkles with thousands of tiny lights.

Holiday River of Lights, New Braunfels; (830) 608–2100. This drive-through lighting park illuminates nearly a mile along Cypress Bend Park, with hundreds of thousands of twinkling lights and holiday scenes. Believed to be the first of its kind in the Southwest, the event features Santas, reindeer, giant Christmas packages, holiday trees, and more. More than thirty large luminous animated displays, such as reindeer leaping over the road, lighted tunnels, holiday trees, and a 15-foot lighted teddy bear, enchant visitors of all ages. While viewing the lights, visitors can tune into an FM radio station to hear the sounds of the holidays as well.

Las Posadas, San Antonio; (800) 447–3372. This beautiful ceremony dramatizes Joseph and Mary's search for an inn with costumed children leading a procession down the River Walk. Holiday music selections are sung in English and Spanish.

Lights Spectacular, Johnson City; (830) 868–7684. One of the biggest displays in the state, this dazzling event features more than 600,000 lights illuminating homes, businesses, and churches, transforming this quiet Hill Country community into a glittering wonderland. The largest light display is on the Blanco County Courthouse, a historic building aglow with more than 100,000 tiny white lights.

Maps available at the courthouse lead you on a self-guided drive by Johnson City's fantastic home light displays, erected by local citizens who play a big part in spreading the holiday spirit. The community also has "light art displays," illuminated panels with up to 1,200 lights. A large Christmas tree in Memorial Park on US 290 is also illuminated with thousands of colored lights.

Wassailfest, New Braunfels; (800) 572–2626. Merchants throughout the downtown area prepare the traditional English holiday drink of wassail and serve it to evening guests, who also enjoy live music, horse and buggy rides, and a visit from Santa. Look for open houses, caroling, and bell choirs on this special evening of holiday fun.

appendix a

entering mexico

The easiest way to enter Mexico is by walking across the International Bridge, or Puente Internacional, for a small toll. On your return, pay another small toll, walk across the bridge, then head through U.S. customs. (See Appendix B, "Shopping in Mexico," for details.) Starting December 31, 2007, you will need a valid U.S. passport to return to the United States after a land crossing into Mexico. For information on obtaining a U.S. passport, see the U.S. Department of State Web site, www.travel.state.gov.

Every border town has taxi service into and out of Mexico. The ride is only a few dollars each way. Call the local chamber of commerce for information on transportation to Mexican shopping areas or dining spots.

Driving into Mexico can be a somewhat frightening prospect because auto mishaps are a criminal rather than civil offense across the border. (If you are in a wreck, you might find yourself in a Mexican jail, a sure way to spoil a vacation.) Short-term Mexican insurance is required of every driver. Your regular car insurance is not valid in Mexico. Every Texas border town has several insurance companies that sell short-term Mexican insurance. Call the local chamber of commerce for information on these companies.

Once you are in Mexico, look for secured parking. The larger restaurants have pay parking lots, and these are preferable to parking on the streets.

Remember that Mexican speed signs are posted in kilometers. Also, Mexican traffic lights are slightly different than those in the United States. When you see a yellow light begin to blink, it means that yellow will soon change to red.

Mexican streets are very narrow and often one-way, especially in the main tourist areas.

appendix b

shopping in mexico

No trip to the Mexican border is complete without some shopping. For many South Texans, this is a chance to purchase quality jewelry, blankets, and liquor at prices far below those in the United States.

All shopping in the border towns is done with American currency. The CASA DE CAMBIO signs are seen on many streets, but you do not need to exchange currency before you go. Most shopkeepers speak fluent English, especially in Nuevo Laredo and Ciudad Acuña. In Piedras Negras, bring along a Spanish-English dictionary if you plan to venture beyond the market area.

Buying is usually done by *negociación*. Many stores do not label items with a price. The shopkeeper names a price, one higher than he or she knows is acceptable. The shopper asks for the "best price," and friendly haggling ensues. Usually both the merchant and the shopper part company happy with the deal.

Making purchases from street vendors is also done through negociación. Street vendors have good prices on paper flowers, hammocks, lace tablecloths, inlaid earrings (not sterling silver), and wood carvings.

Silver jewelry is a hot item in border shops. Look for the "921" stamp on the back of the piece to ensure silver quality. Many of the better stores sell jewelry by weight, with a fixed price per ounce. Even so, silver is very reasonably priced in comparison to that sold in the U.S. stores. You can also get a good bargain on silver and black onyx jewelry.

Glass (especially pitchers, bowls, and blue-rimmed drinking glasses) and leather goods also make excellent purchases. Onyx chess sets, papier-mâché fruits and vegetables, elaborately embroidered Mexican dresses, and woven blankets are other good buys.

Heading home, you must cross through U.S. customs, located on the American side of the International Bridge. Certain items cannot be carried back into the United States. These include fruits, vegetables, animals and birds, and meats (including canned items). Fireworks, switchblade knives (sold by nearly every street vendor), firearms, liquor-filled candy, lottery tickets, and items made from endangered species will be confiscated. Although you can go to the *farmacia* and buy any item without a prescription, you cannot bring it back to the United States. This includes Mexican diet pills, Cipro, and other prescription drugs.

Be careful of counterfeit trademark items, such as $40 Rolex watches sold in many shops. These can be seized, and you must forfeit them if stopped by a customs official.

With both increased NAFTA traffic and tightened border security, lines can be long when returning to the United States, especially for vehicular traffic. During peak times, vehicular border crossings can take hours, although the waiting time is usually shorter.

When you return to the United States, a customs official will ask if you are an American citizen. He or she may ask what you purchased and may also ask to see your purchases and other belongings.

You must also pass by a booth to pay tax on imported liquor and cigarettes. If you are older than twenty-one, you may bring back one liter of liquor and 200 cigarettes. Texas places a tax on both these items, but the savings is still substantial, especially on items like Mexican beer and tequila.

As far as other goods, you may return with $800 worth of merchandise without paying duty. Every person in your party, regardless of age, has this $800 exemption.

If you've made large purchases, save your receipts. You must pay a duty on goods more than $800 (although family members are permitted to combine exemptions).

For more information on customs, obtain Publication 512, "Know Before You Go," by writing U.S. Customs Service, P.O. Box 7407, Washington, DC 20044, or see www.customs .ustreas.gov.

appendix c

especially for winter texans

If you're among the many lucky travelers who've adopted the Lone Star State as their winter home, welcome to Texas. You've chosen a destination where you can enjoy the excitement of the West, the zest of Old Mexico, the tranquillity of the Gulf, and the history of a rambunctious republic, all in one journey. Some of the best seasons and reasons to see the state include the changing post oak leaves in fall, the glittering Christmas festivals, and the often sunny Texas winter days.

To introduce you to winter attractions throughout the state, there's a free publication available called *Winter Texan Magazine.* It includes information on campgrounds, motel discounts for Winter Texans, festivals, and attractions. Call the magazine at (800) 728–1287 or the Texas Department of Transportation at (800) 8888–TEX or (512) 452–9292.

Texas has an excellent network of state parks, most of which provide campsites with hookups. Generally there is a fourteen-consecutive-days limit for camping at each park. The central reservation number for all Texas state parks is (512) 389–8900, 9:00 A.M. to 8:00 P.M. on weekdays and 9:00 A.M. to noon on Saturday. You may also make reservations online at www.tpwd.tx.us/park/admin/res/.

Winter Texans will also be interested in state park passes. The Texas Parklands Passport (which is also called a Bluebonnet Pass) is for those who meet one of these eligibility requirements:

- If you are sixty-five years of age or older and a Texas resident, you can receive 50 percent off entry. Residents and nonresidents who turned sixty-five years before September 1, 1995, are entitled to waived entry fees at state parks.
- Veterans of the U.S. armed services with a 60 percent or more service-connected disability will receive waived entry fees to state parks.
- Travelers who have been medically determined to be permanently disabled as a result of a mental or physical impairment (including blindness) are entitled to 50 percent off entry.

To get this Texas Parklands Passport, you'll need to apply at any state park or at the headquarters in Austin.

If you don't qualify for the Parklands Passport, you can purchase an annual pass called the Texas State Parks Pass. It's valid for twelve months and is presently priced at $60 for a one-car membership or $75 if you would like two cars in the family covered.

appendix d

guide to tex-mex food

You'll find Tex-Mex food everywhere you go in central and southern Texas. It's a staple with all true Texans, who enjoy stuffing themselves at least once a week with baskets of tostadas, a Mexican plate (an enchilada, taco, and rice and beans), and cold *cerveza*. Unlike true Mexican food, which is not unusually spicy and often features seafood, Tex-Mex is heavy, ranges from hot to inedible, and can't be beat.

cabrito—young, tender goat, usually cooked over an open flame on a spit. In border towns, you'll see it hanging it many market windows.

cerveza—beer.

chalupa—a fried, flat corn tortilla spread with refried beans and topped with meat, lettuce, tomatoes, and cheese.

chiles rellenos—stuffed poblano peppers, dipped in batter and deep fried.

enchilada—corn or flour tortillas wrapped around a filling and covered with a hot or mild sauce. The most common varieties are beef, chicken, and cheese. Sour cream and shrimp are sometimes offered.

fajitas—grilled skirt steak strips, wrapped in flour tortillas. Usually served still sizzling on a metal platter, with condiments (*pico de gallo,* sour cream, cheese) on the side.

flautas—corn tortillas wrapped around shredded beef, chicken, or pork and fried until crispy; may be an appetizer or an entree.

frijoles refritos—refried beans.

guacamole—avocado dip spiced with chopped onions, peppers, and herbs.

margarita—popular tequila drink, served in a salted glass; may be served over ice or frozen.

menudo—a soup made from tripe, most popular as a hangover remedy.

mole ("MOLE-ay")—an unusual sauce made of nuts, spices, and chocolate that's served over chicken enchiladas.

picante sauce—a Mexican staple found on most tables, this red sauce is made from peppers and onions and can be eaten as a dip for tortilla chips; ranges from mild to very hot.

pico de gallo—hot sauce made of chopped onions, peppers, and cilantro; used to spice up tacos, chalupas, and fajitas.

quesadillas—tortillas filled and covered with cheese and baked; served as a main dish or an appetizer.

sopapillas—fried pastry dessert served with honey.

tamales—corn dough filled with chopped pork, rolled in a corn shuck, steamed, and then served with or without chile sauce; a very popular Christmas dish.

tortilla—flat cooked rounds of flour or cornmeal used in many main dishes and also eaten like bread along with the meal, with or without butter.

verde—green sauce used as a dip or on enchiladas.

appendix e

texas state parks

Texas has an excellent system of state parks offering camping, fishing, hiking, boating, and tours of historical sites. Facilities range from those with hiking trails, golf courses, and cabins to others that are largely undeveloped and exist as an example of how the region once looked.

Reservations are recommended for overnight facilities. Pets are permitted if they are confined or on a leash shorter than 6 feet and with proof of vaccinations within the past year. The central reservation number for all Texas state parks is (512) 389–8900, Monday through Friday 9:00 A.M. to 8:00 P.M. and Saturday 9:00 A.M. to noon. See www.tpwd.tx.us/park/admin/res for online, e-mail, and fax reservations.

If you are sixty-five or older, a veteran with at least a 60 percent service-related disability, or a frequent state-park visitor, you may want to consider purchasing a Texas Parklands Passport or a Texas State Parks Pass. For details see Appendix C, "Especially for Winter Texans."

For more information on Texas state parks, call the Texas Parks and Wildlife Department at (800) 792–1112, Monday through Friday during working hours, or at (512) 389–8950 in the Austin area. See also www.tpwd.state.tx.us.

appendix f

lcra parks

When it comes to parks, central Texas travelers have only one problem: selecting from a long list of excellent facilities. Many of these parks are the products of the Lower Colorado River Authority (LCRA), a conservation and reclamation district that generates and transmits electricity produced by the powerful Colorado River. The LCRA also manages the waters of the river and assists riverside and lakeside communities with their economic development.

Among travelers, the LCRA is best known for its parks. These sites, which vary from unimproved sites along the riverbanks to full-fledged parks with boat ramps, fishing piers, and camping, are favorite summer destinations. Scattered from the shores of Lake Buchanan down through the rest of the Highland Lakes and along the riverbanks of the Colorado River all the way to Matagorda County on the Gulf Coast, these reservoirs offer vacationers a great place to relax.

For more information on LCRA parks, call (800) 776–5272 or see www.lcra.org.

 # about the authors

John Bigley and Paris Permenter are a husband-wife team of travel writers. Longtime residents of central Texas, they make their home in the Hill Country west of Austin near Lake Travis.

John and Paris write frequently about Texas and other destinations for numerous magazines and newspapers. Their articles and photos have appeared in *Reader's Digest, Texas Highways,* the *Austin American-Statesman,* the *San Antonio Express-News,* and many other publications. They also write a monthly column on day-trip travel for San Antonio's *Fiesta* magazine.

John and Paris's other books include *Shifra Stein's Day Trips from Austin, Insiders' Guide to San Antonio, Adventure Guide to the Cayman Islands, Adventure Guide to the Leeward Islands, Caribbean with Kids, Cayman Islands Alive!, Caribbean for Lovers, Gourmet Getaways, Texas Getaways for Two,* and *Texas Barbecue,* named best regional book by the Mid-America Publishers Association.

Paris and John also edit *Lovetripper.com Romantic Travel Magazine,* an online publication focusing on honeymoons, destination weddings, and romantic resorts around the globe.

Both Paris and John are members of the prestigious Society of American Travel Writers.

More about Paris and John can be found on their Web sites: www.parisandjohn.com and www.lovetripper.com.